Connect

Student's Book

Jack C. Richards
Carlos Barbisan
with **Chuck Sandy**

CAMBRIDGE
UNIVERSITY PRESS

PUBLISHED BY THE PRESS SYNDICATE OF THE UNIVERSITY OF CAMBRIDGE
The Pitt Building, Trumpington Street, Cambridge, United Kingdom

CAMBRIDGE UNIVERSITY PRESS
The Edinburgh Building, Cambridge CB2 2RU, UK
40 West 20th Street, New York, NY 10011–4211, USA
477 Williamstown Road, Port Melbourne, VIC 3207, Australia
Ruiz de Alarcón 13, 28014 Madrid, Spain
Dock House, The Waterfront, Cape Town 8001, South Africa

http://www.cambridge.org

© Cambridge University Press 2004

First published 2004
2nd printing 2004

Printed in Hong Kong, China

Typeface New Century Schoolbook   *System* QuarkXPress®

ISBN 0 521 59498 7 Student's Book 1 (English)
ISBN 0 521 60074 X Student's Book 1 (Portuguese)
ISBN 0 521 59495 2 Workbook 1 (English)
ISBN 0 521 60070 7 Workbook 1 (Portuguese)
ISBN 0 521 59494 4 Teacher's Edition 1 (English)
ISBN 0 521 59492 8 Teacher's Edition 1 (Portuguese)
ISBN 0 521 59491 X Class Audio Cassettes 1
ISBN 0 521 59488 X Class CD 1
ISBN 0 521 59487 1 Student's Book 2 (English)
ISBN 0 521 60073 1 Student's Book 2 (Portuguese)
ISBN 0 521 59484 7 Workbook 2 (English)
ISBN 0 521 60069 3 Workbook 2 (Portuguese)
ISBN 0 521 59493 6 Teacher's Edition 2 (English)
ISBN 0 521 59481 2 Teacher's Edition 2 (Portuguese)
ISBN 0 521 59480 4 Class Audio Cassettes 2
ISBN 0 521 59477 4 Class CD 2

ISBN 0 521 59476 6 Student's Book 3 (English)
ISBN 0 521 60072 3 Student's Book 3 (Portuguese)
ISBN 0 521 59475 8 Workbook 3 (English)
ISBN 0 521 60068 5 Workbook 3 (Portuguese)
ISBN 0 521 59483 9 Teacher's Edition 3 (English)
ISBN 0 521 59474 X Teacher's Edition 3 (Portuguese)
ISBN 0 521 59473 1 Class Audio Cassettes 3
ISBN 0 521 59471 5 Class CD 3
ISBN 0 521 59470 7 Student's Book 4 (English)
ISBN 0 521 60071 5 Student's Book 4 (Portuguese)
ISBN 0 521 59469 3 Workbook 4 (English)
ISBN 0 521 60064 2 Workbook 4 (Portuguese)
ISBN 0 521 59482 0 Teacher's Edition 4 (English)
ISBN 0 521 59468 5 Teacher's Edition 4 (Portuguese)
ISBN 0 521 59467 7 Class Audio Cassettes 4
ISBN 0 521 59464 2 Class CD 4

Book design, art direction, and layout services: Adventure House, NYC

Table of Contents

SYLLABUS

Unit 1 – All About You and Me

Lesson	Function	Grammar	Vocabulary	Theme Project
Lesson 1 New friends	Asking about others	Negative statements / Questions with the verb *be*	Name, age, country of origin, likes	Make a poster about your likes and dislikes.
Lesson 2 Neighborhoods	Describing your neighborhood	*There is / There are… Is there a / Are there any…?*	Recreational, commercial, and public places	
Lesson 3 Talents	Describing someone's talents	*be good at*	Talents	
Lesson 4 Our pets	Talking about likes and dislikes	*like + a lot / very much / a little don't like + very much / at all*	Animals and adjectives to describe them	
Lesson 5 Connections	Reading • Listening Writing			

Unit 2 – Our Lives and Routines

Lesson	Function	Grammar	Vocabulary	Theme Project
Lesson 6 School days	Describing daily routines	Simple present statements with *I*	Daily routines	Make a routine chart for a person in another class.
Lesson 7 Free time	Asking about free-time activities	*Do you + (verb)…?*	Free-time activities	
Lesson 8 People I admire	Talking about people's lives	Simple present statements with *I / he / she*	Activities	
Lesson 9 The weekend	Talking about weekend activities	*doesn't*	Weekend activities	
Lesson 10 Connections	Reading • Listening Writing			

Unit 3 – Sports and Activities

Lesson	Function	Grammar	Vocabulary	Theme Project
Lesson 11 Sports fun	Asking what sports someone does	*Does he / she…?*	Sports verbs	Make a sports card.
Lesson 12 Sports equipment	Talking about sports equipment	*They + verb: statements Do they + verb: questions*	Sports equipment	
Lesson 13 Off to camp	Talking about rules	Imperatives	Camp supplies	
Lesson 14 At camp	Talking about when activities happen	*What time / When…?*	Camp activities	
Lesson 15 Connections	Reading • Listening Writing			

Unit 4 – My Interests

Lesson	Function	Grammar	Vocabulary	Theme Project
Lesson 16 I like music.	Talking about music preferences	*her / him / it / them*	Types of music	Make a song poster.
Lesson 17 Let's look online.	Asking about prices	*How much is / are…?*	Items in a natural science catalog	
Lesson 18 Our interests	Talking about free-time activities	*like / don't like + to* (verb)	Free-time activities and interests	
Lesson 19 In and out of school	Talking about habits and routines	Adverbs of frequency	Habits and daily activities	
Lesson 20 Connections	Reading • Listening Writing			

Unit 5 – Favorite Activities

Lesson	Function	Grammar	Vocabulary	Theme Project
Lesson 21 In San Francisco	Describing vacation activities	Present continuous affirmative statements	Vacation activities	Make a city guide for tourists.
Lesson 22 At the park	Describing how someone is not following rules	Present continuous negative statements	Rules at a park	
Lesson 23 At the beach	Asking what someone is doing	Present continuous *Yes / No* questions	Beach activities	
Lesson 24 At the store	Asking what someone is doing	Present continuous *What* questions	Store items	
Lesson 25 Connections	Reading • Listening Writing			

Unit 6 – Entertainment

Lesson	Function	Grammar	Vocabulary	Theme Project
Lesson 26 Where are you going?	Asking where someone is going	*Where + (be) . . . going?*	Entertainment events and adjectives to describe them	Make a group guide of favorite weekend activities.
Lesson 27 Birthday parties!	Talking about special events	Simple present vs. present continuous	Favorite birthday activities	
Lesson 28 Let's see a movie.	Talking about types of movies to see	*want / don't want + to* (verb)	Types of movies	
Lesson 29 In line at the movies	Asking what someone looks like	*What* questions about people	Adjectives to describe appearance	
Lesson 30 Connections	Reading • Listening Writing			

Unit 7 – What We Eat

Lesson	Function	Grammar	Vocabulary	Theme Project
Lesson 31 I'm hungry!	Talking about food	Countable and uncountable nouns	Food	Make a group menu.
Lesson 32 Picnic plans	Asking about quantities	*How much / How many . . . ?*	Picnic foods and utensils	
Lesson 33 A snack	Planning menus	*some / any*	Condiments	
Lesson 34 On the menu	Ordering from a menu	*would like*	Menu items	
Lesson 35 Connections	Reading • Listening Writing			

Unit 8 – The Natural World

Lesson	Function	Grammar	Vocabulary	Theme Project
Lesson 36 World weather	Talking about the weather	*What's the weather like?*	Adjectives to describe the weather	Make an informational guide about a different continent.
Lesson 37 Natural wonders	Talking about outdoor activities	*can* (for possibility)	Water and land forms	
Lesson 38 World of friends	Asking who does different activities	*Who + (verb) . . . ?*	Languages and countries	
Lesson 39 International Day	Asking about personal information	*What + (noun) . . . ?*	Numbers 101+	
Lesson 40 Connections	Reading • Listening Writing			

New friends

1. Vocabulary review

A Read about the new students at Kent International School. Then listen and practice.

New Students at Kent International School

I'm Zach. I'm from the U.S., and I'm 12. I like baseball and volleyball.

Hello. I'm from Puerto Rico. My name is Ana, and I'm 13. I like movies and concerts.

My name is Tommy. I'm from Australia. I like music and comic books. I'm 13.

Hi. I'm Kate. I'm 13. I'm from Canada. I like computers and math.

Hello there! My name is Claudia. I'm 13. I'm from Colombia. My favorite sports are Ping-Pong and tennis.

My name is Rafael. I'm from Brazil. I like soccer and video games. I'm 13.

B Complete the chart with information from part A.

Name	Age	Place	Likes
1. _Claudia_	_13_	_Colombia_	_Ping-Pong and tennis_
2. _____	___	_Brazil_	_____
3. _____	___	_the U.S._	_____
4. _____	___	_____	_computers and math_
5. _____	___	_Puerto Rico_	_____
6. _____	_13_	_____	_____

2. Language focus review

A Review the language in the chart.

Negative statements / Questions with the verb *be*		
She**'s not** my art teacher.	They**'re not** my classmates.	My name**'s not** Anita.

Who's she?
  She**'s** my math teacher.
	Who are they?
	  They**'re** my friends.
		What's your name?
		  My name**'s** Ana.

It**'s not** in July.	It**'s not** in Brazil.	I**'m not** from São Paulo.

When's your birthday?
  It**'s** in November.
	Where's San Juan?
	  It**'s** in Puerto Rico.
		Where are you from?
		  I**'m** from San Juan.

He**'s not** fourteen.	**Is he nice?**
	  Yes, he **is**.
	  No, he**'s not**.
		Are you in her class?
		  Yes, I **am**.
		  No, I**'m not**.

How old is he? He**'s** thirteen.		

🔊 **B** Complete the conversation. Listen and check. Then practice.

Zach Hi. _What's_ (What's / Where's) your name?

Ana My name's Ana. _____ (I'm / He's) from San Juan.

Zach Hi, Ana. My name's Zach. So, _____ (who's / where's) San Juan? _____ (Is / Are) it in Brazil?

Ana No, _____ (it's / it's not). It's in Puerto Rico.

Zach Oh, right. How old _____ (is / are) you, Ana?

Ana I'm thirteen. My birthday is in May. _____ (Where's / When's) your birthday?

Zach It's in June. Hey, _____ (who's / what's) she?

Ana _____ (They're / She's) my math teacher, Mrs. Archer.

Zach _____ (Are / Is) you in Ms. Kelley's science class?

Ana No, _____ (She's not / I'm not). I'm in Mr. Perez's class.

Zach _____ (Is / Are) he nice?

Ana Yes, he is. Actually, _____ (I'm / he's) my father.

3. Speaking

Play a game. Think of a place, a country, a hobby, or a school subject. Give clues. Your classmates guess.

You It's a country. It's not the U.S.

Classmate 1 Is it Peru?

You No, it's not.

Classmate 2 Is it Canada?

You Yes, it is!

Lesson 2 Neighborhoods

1. Language focus review

◁)) What are Rafael's and Tommy's neighborhoods like? Look at the pictures, and complete the sentences. Then listen and check.

There is / There are . . .
There's a park. / **There's no** park.
There are basketball courts. / **There are no** basketball courts.

Is there a / Are there any . . . ?
Is there a mall?
Yes, **there is.** / No, **there isn't.**
Are there any stores?
Yes, **there are.** / No, **there aren't.**

Rafael's neighborhood

Tommy's neighborhood

Rafael's neighborhood

1. _There's a_ _____ beautiful park.
2. _____ tennis courts.
3. _____ basketball courts.

Tommy's neighborhood

4. _____ gym.
5. _____ many stores.
6. _____ big mall.

2. Listening

◁)) What other places are in Tommy's neighborhood?
Listen and check (✓) the correct places.

✓ music store

☐ video arcade

☐ park

☐ basketball court

☐ swimming pool

☐ library

☐ school

☐ bookstore

3. Speaking

A Complete survey questions 1–6 with *Is there a* or *Are there any*.
Write questions 7 and 8 with your classmates.

B Complete the survey for yourself. Then ask a classmate
the questions.

Neighborhood Survey	You		Your classmate	
	Yes	No	Yes	No
1. _Is there a_ school?	☐	☐	☐	☐
2. _____ movie theaters?	☐	☐	☐	☐
3. _____ swimming pool?	☐	☐	☐	☐
4. _____ mall?	☐	☐	☐	☐
5. _____ restaurants?	☐	☐	☐	☐
6. _____ library?	☐	☐	☐	☐
7. _____	☐	☐	☐	☐
8. _____	☐	☐	☐	☐

Is there a school in
your neighborhood?

Yes, there is.

C Tell your classmates about your neighborhood.
Use the words below or your own ideas.

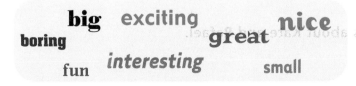

big   exciting   nice
boring   great
fun   interesting   small

There's a big music store in my
neighborhood. There are...

1. Language check

A Read Kate's and Rafael's bulletin boards. Then write questions and answers.

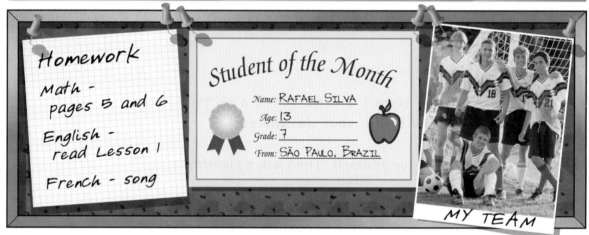

1. **Q:** _Where's Kate from?_

   A: She's from Canada.

2. **Q:** Is Rafael from Brazil?

   A: _____

3. **Q:** Are Rafael and Kate in the same French class?

   A: _____

4. **Q:** How old is Kate?

   A: _____

5. **Q:** _____

   A: He's thirteen.

6. **Q:** Where's São Paulo?

   A: _____

7. **Q:** Is Kate from Canada?

   A: _____

8. **Q:** _____

   A: It's in Canada.

B Now ask and answer questions about Kate and Rafael.

> Is Kate thirteen?   Yes, she is.

2. Game What's Wrong?

Work with a classmate. What's wrong with the picture? Write sentences with the words in the box. The pair that finishes first is the winner.

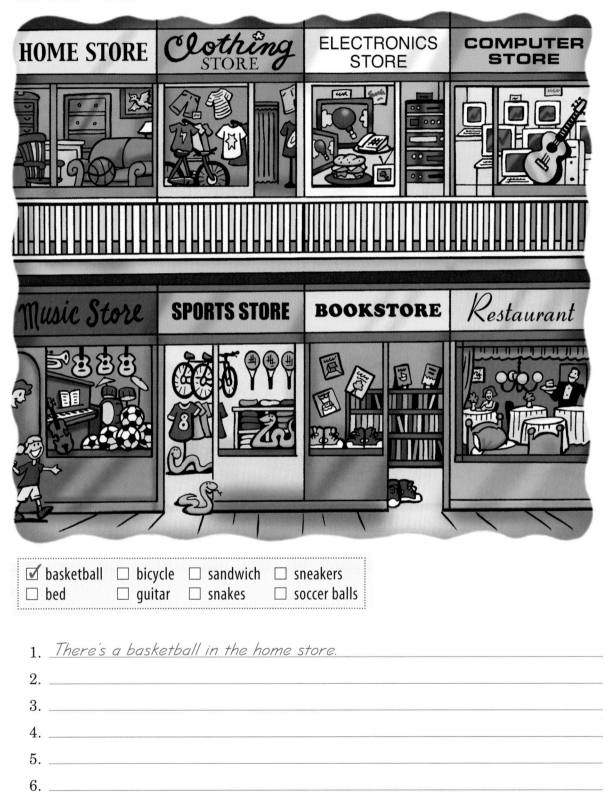

| ☑ basketball | ☐ bicycle | ☐ sandwich | ☐ sneakers |
| ☐ bed | ☐ guitar | ☐ snakes | ☐ soccer balls |

1. _There's a basketball in the home store._

2. _____

3. _____

4. _____

5. _____

6. _____

7. _____

8. _____

1. Vocabulary

🔊 **What are these students' talents? Write the sentences below the correct people. Then listen and practice.**

☐ She's artistic.	☐ She's friendly.	☐ He's musical.
☐ She's athletic.	☑ He's funny.	☐ He's smart.

1. He can tell jokes.
   He's funny.

2. She can make friends easily.

3. He can speak three languages.

4. She can play a lot of sports.

5. He can play a lot of instruments.

6. She can draw great pictures.

2. Listening

🔊 **A What do you think these students can do? Listen and check (✓) the correct activities.**

1. Silvio: ☐ He can play basketball.   ☐ He can play video games.
2. Beth: ☐ She can play the guitar.   ☐ She can play volleyball.
3. Tony: ☐ He can speak a lot of languages.   ☐ He can dance.
4. Lina: ☐ She can play soccer.   ☐ She can draw.

B Look at your answers to part A. Write the word that describes each student.

1. _athletic_   2. _____   3. _____   4. _____

3. Language focus

be good at

You're **good at** soccer.
He's **pretty good at** soccer.
Tommy's **not good at** soccer.

👍👍 good at
👍 pretty good at
👎 not good at

Tommy's = Tommy is

🔊 **A** Who is good at soccer? Listen and practice.

Kate Hey, Claudia! You're good at soccer! You're really athletic!

Claudia Thanks.

Kate Who's that?

Claudia That's Zach.

Kate He's pretty good at soccer.

Claudia Yeah.

Kate Oh, no! Who's that?

Claudia Uh, that's Tommy. He's not good at soccer.

Kate No. But he can play a lot of instruments. He's very musical.

B What are you good at? Write sentences. Use the words below or your own ideas.

> **Subjects:** English history
> math science art
> **Sports:** volleyball soccer
> tennis basketball

(good at) _I'm good at English._

1. (good at) _____

2. (pretty good at) _____

3. (not good at) _____

C What are different students in your class good at? Tell your classmates.

> Heather is good at volleyball.

4. Pronunciation Stress

🔊 Listen. Notice the stress in the sentences. Then listen again and practice.

I'm **good** at drawing. I'm **artistic**.	I'm **not** good at drawing. I'm **not** artistic.
I'm **good** at sports. I'm **athletic**.	I'm **not** good at sports. I'm **not** athletic.
He's **good** at the guitar. He's **musical**.	He's **not** good at the guitar. He's **not** musical.

All About You and Me 9

4 Our pets

1. Vocabulary

🔊 **A** Students describe their pets at the school pet show. Match the students to the correct texts. Then listen and practice.

☐ Mopsy and Flopsy are boring. They're my brother's rabbits.

☐ Bootsie is my cat. She's my favorite pet. She's really cute.

☐ Mac is my dog. He's very active. I love dogs.

☐ Max and Mo are my two spiders. They're very interesting.

☐ *1* Jambu is our parrot. She can speak English. She's messy.

☐ I like my snake. His name is George. He's not dangerous.

B Which animals in part A do you think are good pets? Which are bad pets? Complete the chart. Then tell your classmates.

Good pets	Why	Bad pets	Why
dogs	*cute*		

> Dogs are good pets. They're cute.

2. Language focus

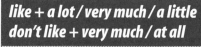

A Celia shows Todd the animals at the pet show. Listen and practice.

like + a lot / very much / a little
don't like + very much / at all

 I like cats **a lot.**
I like rabbits **very much.**
 I like dogs **a little.**
I don't like spiders **very much.**
I don't like snakes **at all.**

Celia Hey, Todd. Look at the cute cat. I like cats a lot!

Todd You do? I don't like cats very much. They're boring.

Celia But you like dogs, right?

Todd Yeah, they're really friendly.

Celia Well, I like dogs a little.

Todd Wow! Look at that snake over there.

Celia Ugh! I don't like snakes at all. They're dangerous.

B Complete these sentences with the correct words. Then listen and check.

1. Rabbits are boring. I don't like rabbits _____*at all*_____ (a little / at all).
2. Parrots are OK. I like parrots _____ (at all / a little).
3. Cats aren't very nice. I don't like cats _____ (a little / very much).
4. Dogs are cute. I like dogs _____ (a lot / at all).
5. Snakes are very bad pets. I don't like snakes _____ (a little / at all).
6. Spiders are interesting. I like spiders _____ (at all / very much).

3. Speaking

Play a chain game. Learn what animals your classmates like and don't like.

Leah I like dogs a lot. How about you, Mario?
Mario I like dogs a little.
    → **Mario** I don't like cats at all. How about you, Yumi?
        Yumi I like cats very much.
            → **Yumi** I don't like . . .

1. Reading

What's your hobby?

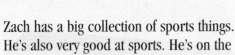

Tommy has a huge collection of comic books. Some of his comic books are very old. There are always a lot of students at his table on Hobby Day. Zach says, "Tommy's collection is cool."

There are almost 75 CDs in Ana's collection. She has music from many countries. A lot of her CDs are from Puerto Rico. "The flamenco CD from Spain is my favorite," says Claudia.

Zach has a big collection of sports things. He's also very good at sports. He's on the baseball team. He can also play soccer. Zach says, "I like a lot of sports, but I don't like tennis very much. It's boring."

Kate is really good at computers. She can draw great pictures, too. You can see her pictures on her Web site. "Kate's Web site is beautiful and interesting," says Rafael.

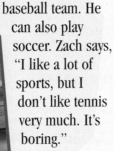

A Read the article about Hobby Day.

B Who is each sentence about? Write *Tommy, Ana, Zach,* or *Kate.*

1. Students listen to music at her table. _____

2. This student is really athletic. _____

3. This student is artistic. _____

4. Students read at his table. _____

2. Listening

🔊 Listen to an interview with Ivis, another student at Hobby Day.
Are these sentences true or false? Check (✓) T (true) or F (false).

	T	F
1. Ivis is 13.	☐	☑
2. Ivis's birthday is on Thursday.	☐	☐
3. Ivis is from Peru.	☐	☐
4. Ivis has a collection of video games.	☐	☐
5. Ivis is pretty good at the guitar.	☐	☐
6. Ivis's favorite music is rock.	☐	☐

3. Writing

A Complete the web about one of your friends.

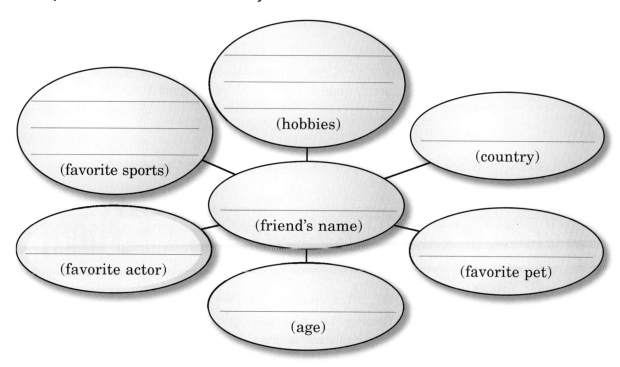

(hobbies)

(favorite sports)

(country)

(favorite actor)

(friend's name)

(favorite pet)

(age)

B Write an article about your friend. Use part A to help you.

My friend's name is . . .

Review

Language chart review

The verb be

Wh- and How questions	Statements	Yes / No questions	Short answers
Where are you from?	I'm from Brazil. I'm not from Peru.	Are you in my class?	Yes, I am. No, I'm not.
How old is she?	She's twelve. She's not thirteen.	Is he from Australia?	Yes, he is. No, he's not.
Where are you?	We're at the mall. We're not at the park.	Are you brothers?	Yes, we are. No, we're not.
Who are they?	They're my friends. They're not my sisters.	Are they fun?	Yes, they are. No, they're not.
is not = isn't / 's not	are not = aren't / are not		

be good at

You're good at sports.   Jason's pretty good at music.   We're not good at science.

Jason's = Jason is

A Nick, Andy, and Sonia are in a new TV show. Complete the sentences.

Meet the kids from Central HIGH SCHOOL

My ___name's___ (name / name's) Nick Lake. _____ (I'm / He's) on a cool, new television show on Teen TV. The show is called *Central High School*. My friends and I _____ (am / are) students at Central High School. Central High School _____ (is / are) in Riverside City.

_____ (This is / These are) my friends. This is Andy. Andy's _____ (good is / good at) art. _____ (He's / She's) not good at math. _____ (They're / We're) in the same math class. Our teacher _____ (isn't / aren't) happy with Andy.

Say hello to Sonia. _____ (He's / She's) not from Riverside. _____ (She's / We're) Andy's cousin from Brazil. _____ (She / She's) pretty and very smart. Sonia's _____ (pretty good / is pretty) at sports, too.

B Write questions with the correct forms of *be*. Then look again at part A, and answer the questions.

1. Nick's last name / Lake

   Q: *Is Nick's last name Lake?*   **A:** *Yes, it is.*

2. where / Central High School

   Q: _____   **A:** _____

3. who / Andy and Sonia

   Q: _____   **A:** _____

4. Sonia / good at sports

   Q: _____   **A:** _____

Language chart review

There is / There are . . .	
There's a tennis court.	**There's no** basketball court.
There are restaurants.	**There are no** movie theaters.
	There aren't any movie theaters.
Is there a mall?	**Are there any** music stores?
Yes, there is. / No, there isn't.	Yes, there are. / No, there aren't.

a lot / very much a little / not at all
I **like** science **a lot**.
I **like** geography **a little**.
I **don't like** math **very much**.
I **don't like** P.E. **at all**.

C Dan and Sue are at a pet store. Complete the conversation with *are*, *is*, *there's*, and *they're*.

Dan There _____ *are* _____ a lot of animals here!

Sue I know. _____ there a parrot?

Dan Yes, there _____ . Look!

Sue Oh, it's beautiful! And _____ a very cute cat.

Dan Cats aren't friendly.

Sue Oh, cats aren't bad. Look! _____ a black spider.

Dan Ugh! I don't like spiders at all. _____ there any dogs?

Sue Yes, there _____ . _____ in front of you.

D What do you think Dan and Sue say? Look again at part C. Then write sentences with *like* or *don't like*.

1. (parrots / a lot)   **Sue** *I like parrots a lot.*

2. (cats / a little)   **Sue** _____

3. (cats / at all)   **Dan** _____

4. (dogs / a lot)   **Dan** _____

School days

1. Vocabulary

A Read about Pam's day. Then listen and practice.

6:00 AM

Every day, I get up at 6:00 in the morning.

6:35 AM

I eat breakfast at home.

7:00 AM

Then I go to school with my brother.

12:30 PM

I eat lunch with my friends in the cafeteria.

4:00 PM

At 4:00, I go home.

4:30 PM

Then I do my homework.

7:30 PM

At 7:30, I eat dinner with my family.

8:00 PM

Then I watch TV.

10:00 PM

I go to bed at 10:00.

B Imagine you are Pam. Complete her sentences with the correct words from part A.

1. I _____*get up*_____ at 6:00 A.M.

2. I _____ at 8:00 P.M.

3. I _____ at 6:35 A.M.

4. I _____ at 4:30 P.M.

5. I _____ at 12:30 P.M.

16

2. Language focus

A How are Claude's and Keiko's days different from Pam's? Listen and practice.

Simple present statements with *I*
I eat lunch at home.
I don't eat lunch at school.
don't = do not

> I don't eat lunch at school.
> I eat lunch at home.
> I don't go to school with my brother.
> I go to school with my friends.

Claude – France

> I don't go home after school.
> I go home after my violin lesson.
> I don't go to bed at 10:00.
> I go to bed at 11:00.

Keiko – Japan

B How about you? Is your day like Pam's day? Write sentences.

(get up at 6:00) *I get up at 6:00, too.* OR *I don't get up at 6:00. I get up at 7:00.*

1. (eat lunch with my friends) _____

2. (eat in the cafeteria) _____

3. (go home at 4:00) _____

4. (go to bed at 10:00) _____

C Now tell your classmates how your day is different from Pam's day.

> I don't get up at 6:00. I get up at 7:00.

3. Listening

Claudia talks about her day. What does she say?
Listen and check (✓) the correct information.

1. I get up at   ☑ 7:00 A.M.   ☐ 8:00 A.M.
2. I go to school at   ☐ 8:30 A.M.   ☐ 9:00 A.M.
3. I eat lunch at   ☐ school.   ☐ home.
4. I go home at   ☐ 2:30.   ☐ 3:45.
5. I watch TV with   ☐ my brother.   ☐ my sister.

7 Free time

1. Vocabulary

🔊 **A** Who does these free-time activities? Write *K* (Kate), *R* (Rafael), or *A* (Ana). Then listen and practice.

I collect stamps. _R_	I listen to music. ___	I take dance lessons. ___
I hang out at the mall. ___	I play video games. ___	I use the Internet. ___
I in-line skate. ___	I talk on the phone. ___	I watch videos and DVDs. ___

Kate

Rafael

Ana

B What do you do in your free time? Write two things you do and two things you don't do.

Things I do	Things I don't do
_I . . ._	_I don't . . ._

2. Language focus

Do you collect trading cards?
Yes, I do.
No, I don't.

🔊 Kate and Rafael take a survey. Complete the conversation. Listen and check. Then practice.

Kate Oh, look! A survey!

Rafael Cool. Let's take it.

Kate Um, do you collect trading cards?

Rafael Yes, I do.

Kate OK. . . . Do you take piano lessons?

Rafael No, I don't.

Kate _____Do_____ you _____use_____ the Internet?

Rafael Yes, _____ .

Kate _____ you _____ TV?

Rafael No, _____ . But I watch videos.

Kate _____ you _____ to music?

Rafael _____ , I do. My favorite singer is Jennifer Lopez.

Kate _____ you _____ video games?

Rafael _____ , _____ . I play video games every weekend.

3. Speaking

A Read the survey. Write questions 8 and 9 with your classmates.

B Complete the survey for yourself. Then ask a classmate the questions.

What do you do in your free time?	You		Your classmate	
	Yes	No	Yes	No
1. Do you use the Internet?	☐	☐	☐	☐
2. Do you collect stamps?	☐	☐	☐	☐
3. Do you listen to music?	☐	☐	☐	☐
4. Do you play video games?	☐	☐	☐	☐
5. Do you talk on the phone?	☐	☐	☐	☐
6. Do you hang out at the mall?	☐	☐	☐	☐
7. Do you collect trading cards?	☐	☐	☐	☐
8. _____	☐	☐	☐	☐
9. _____	☐	☐	☐	☐

Do you use the Internet?   No, I don't.

Mini-review

1. Language check

A Freddy is an alien. He talks about his day. What does he say?
Write sentences.

I get up at 7:00 A.M.

B You are going to interview Freddy. Look at part A, and write four
questions you can ask. Then act out the interview with a classmate.

1.	
2.	
3.	
4.	

You	Do you get up at 7:00 A.M.?
Classmate	Yes, I do.
You	Do you play soccer at 7:00 P.M.?
Classmate	No, I don't. I play soccer at 3:15 P.M.

2. Game Who Is It?

Read what these students do in their free time. Then play a game with a classmate.

Classmate 1 Choose a person below. Don't tell your classmate. Answer Classmate 2's questions.

Classmate 2 Classmate 1 is thinking of a person below. Ask Classmate 1 questions. Guess the person.

Classmate 1 I watch TV.
Classmate 2 Are you Lucy?
Classmate 1 No, I'm not.
Classmate 2 Do you take dance lessons?
Classmate 1 Yes, I do.
Classmate 2 Are you Eric?
Classmate 1 Yes, I am.

Jack: I take dance lessons. I use the Internet. I hang out at the mall. I talk on the phone.

Lucy: I watch TV. I take dance lessons. I listen to music. I talk on the phone.

Justin: I read magazines. I use the Internet. I listen to music. I play computer games.

Eric: I watch TV. I take dance lessons. I in-line skate. I hang out at the mall.

Angela: I watch TV. I collect stamps. I play computer games. I talk on the phone.

Carol: I collect stamps. I use the Internet. I take dance lessons. I listen to music.

Lesson 8 People I admire

1. Vocabulary

🔊 Tommy admires his brother, Jordan. What does Jordan say about his life? Match the photos to the correct sentences. Then listen and practice.

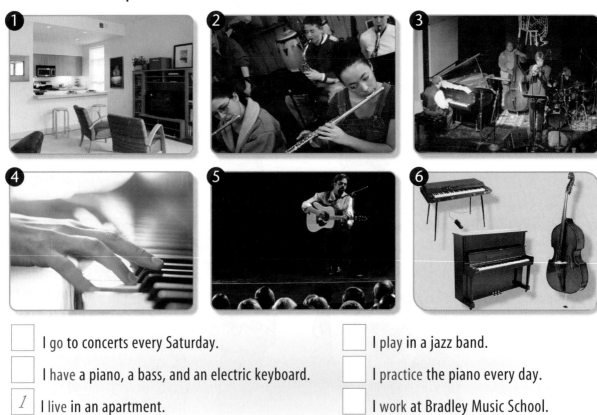

	I go to concerts every Saturday.
	I have a piano, a bass, and an electric keyboard.
1	I live in an apartment.

	I play in a jazz band.
	I practice the piano every day.
	I work at Bradley Music School. I teach music to high school students.

2. Language focus

🔊 **A** Read what Tommy says. Study the language chart. Then listen and practice.

My brother, Jordan, is great. He works at Bradley Music School. He teaches the piano to students from all over the world. Jordan has a piano in his apartment, and he practices every day. At night, he plays in jazz clubs. He really loves music!

Simple present statements with *I*/*he*/*she*					
With *he* and *she*, add *-s* or *-es* to most verbs.					Exception
I live	I work	I teach	I do	I go	I have
he lives	he works	he teaches	he does	he goes	he has
she lives	she works	she teaches	she does	she goes	she has

◁)) **B** Tommy also admires Esteban Cortazar. Complete Tommy's text with the correct forms of the verbs. Then listen and check.

I admire Esteban Cortazar. He's from Colombia, but he _____ (live) in Miami. Esteban is a fashion designer. He's talented, and he _____ (work) hard. He _____ (make) clothes for department stores. He _____ (go) to fashion shows, and he sees his own clothing!

3. Listening

◁)) Skating star Sarah Hughes is another person Tommy admires. Are these sentences true or false? Listen and write *T* (true) or *F* (false).

1. Sarah Hughes is American. ___*T*___

2. She has two brothers and a sister. _____

3. She lives in San Francisco. _____

4. She practices four days a week. _____

5. She listens to music in her free time. _____

6. She plays the violin. _____

4. Pronunciation -*s* endings

◁)) **A** Listen. Notice the -*s* endings. Then listen again and practice.

s = /s/	s = /z/	s = /ɪz/
takes	plays	practices
collects	goes	guesses

◁)) **B** Listen. Write these verbs in the correct columns: *lives, works, teaches, eats, watches,* and *has.*

s = /s/	s = /z/	s = /ɪz/
_____	_____	_____
_____	_____	_____

Lesson 9 The weekend

1. Vocabulary

🔊 **A** What do you do on the weekend? Check (✓) the correct boxes. Then listen and practice.

1. ☐ I sleep late.
   ☐ I don't sleep late.

2. ☐ I eat out with my family.
   ☐ I don't eat out with my family.

3. ☐ I stay up late.
   ☐ I don't stay up late.

4. ☐ I go out on Friday night.
   ☐ I don't go out on Friday night.

5. ☐ I go to the movies.
   ☐ I don't go to the movies.

6. ☐ I stay home on Sunday.
   ☐ I don't stay home on Sunday.

B Tell your classmates about your weekend. Use sentences from part A.

> I sleep late. I eat out with my family. I don't . . .

2. Language focus

🔊 **A** Ana and her sister, Clara, do different things on the weekend. Listen and practice.

My sister and I are very different. On the weekend, I go out with my friends. I go to the movies, or I go to a concert. Clara doesn't go out at all. She stays home and watches videos. On Sunday, I don't sleep late. I get up at 7:30 A.M. Clara sleeps late. She gets up at 10:30 A.M.

doesn't
She doesn't go out on Friday night.
Clara doesn't go out at all.
doesn't = does not

B Rafael and his brother, Luis, are different, too. Look at the photos. Are these sentences true or false? Write *T* (true) or *F* (false).

1. Luis goes out with his parents. ___*F*___

2. Luis goes to concerts. _____

3. Rafael stays home. _____

4. Rafael goes to bed early. _____

5. Rafael watches videos in the living room. _____

6. Luis likes popcorn. _____

11:30 P.M.

Rafael

C Correct the false sentences in part B. Then listen and check.

1. *Luis doesn't go out with his parents.*
   He goes out with his friends.

2. _____

   _____

3. _____

   _____

4. _____

   _____

POPCORN

Luis

3. Speaking

A Read the survey. Write questions 7 and 8 with your classmates.

B Ask a classmate the questions.

What do you do on the weekend?	Your classmate	
	Yes	No
1. Do you sleep late?	☐	☐
2. Do you stay home?	☐	☐
3. Do you go to the movies?	☐	☐
4. Do you do your homework?	☐	☐
5. Do you go out with friends?	☐	☐
6. Do you play video games?	☐	☐
7. _____	☐	☐
8. _____	☐	☐

C Tell the class about your classmate's weekend activities.

> Carla eats out. She doesn't sleep late. She . . .

1. Reading

How do you spend your days?

Homeschool

Anna Kulczyk is 13. She's from Ontario, Canada. Anna studies every day. But she doesn't go to school! Anna is a homeschooler. She studies at home.

Anna uses the Internet a lot. She takes classes online. Of course, Anna does homework. She sends her homework to her teachers by e-mail. After "school," Anna paints pictures, writes stories, and practices the piano and the guitar. She plays with her pet rabbit, too. She also writes an online magazine for other homeschoolers.

But Anna doesn't stay home every day. She has a part-time job at the library. She works there two days a week. She also takes music and karate lessons. Anna likes drama. Sometimes she's in plays.

On weekends, Anna hangs out with her friends. They go shopping, or they go to the park. Anna doesn't go to "school," but she isn't bored or lonely. She has a lot of fun.

A Read the article.

B Are these sentences true or false? Write *T* (true) or *F* (false). Then correct the false sentences.

1. Anna is 12. _____F_____

   She's not 12. She's 13. _____

2. She is American. _____

   _____

3. She takes classes online. _____

   _____

4. She practices the piano and the violin. _____

   _____

5. She has a part-time job at the library. _____

   _____

6. She works at her job five days a week. _____

   _____

7. On weekends, Anna is bored and lonely. _____

   _____

2. Listening

🔊 Anna talks to her friend about her schedule. Listen and check (✓) the correct times.

1. Anna gets up at ☐ 6:30. ☑ 8:00.
2. She goes to her music lesson at ☐ 9:00. ☐ 9:30.
3. She comes home at ☐ 9:30. ☐ 10:30.
4. She eats lunch at ☐ 12:00. ☐ different times.
5. She goes to the library from ☐ 12:30 to 2:00. ☐ 12:00 to 2:30.
6. She eats dinner at ☐ 6:00. ☐ 7:00.
7. She goes to her karate class at ☐ 7:00. ☐ 7:30.
8. She goes to bed at ☐ 11:30. ☐ different times.

3. Writing

A Look at the web about Anna. Think of a person who does interesting things. Use the words in the box or your own ideas to complete the web about the person.

collect   eat   go   hang out   have   play   read   take   use   watch   work   write

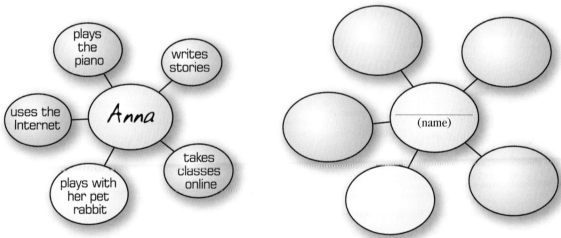

B Now use your web to write an article about the person.

Anna does a lot of things. She uses the Internet. She takes classes online. She writes stories. She also plays the piano. She plays with her pet rabbit, too.

Lessons 6–10 Review

Language chart review

Simple present		
Statements: *I / He / She*	*Yes / No* questions: *Do you . . . ?*	Short answers
I take piano lessons. **I don't take** violin lessons. **He lives** in an apartment. **He doesn't live** in a house. **She gets up** late. **She doesn't get up** early.	**Do you take** piano lessons?	**Yes, I do.** **No, I don't.**
doesn't = does not		

A Carly writes a fan letter to Enrique Iglesias. Complete
Carly's letter and Enrique's reply. Use the correct forms of
the verbs in the box.

do	don't live	listen to	sing
doesn't have	have	live	

Dear Enrique,

How are you? This letter is from my
grandmother and me. I ___*have*___
all your CDs. My grandmother
___*doesn't have*___ your CDs, but she
_____ all of your father's
music. Your father, Julio, is her favorite
singer. She _____ his music
every day. Can you please answer
some questions?

_____ you _____ in
Spain? _____ you
_____ any brothers and
sisters? _____ you
_____ in English and in
Spanish?

You're the best!

Love,
Carly

Dear Carly,

Hi! Here are pictures of my dad and me.
No, I _____ in Spain. I
_____ in the U.S. – in Miami,
Florida. Yes, I _____ a big family.
I have two brothers and three sisters! Yes,
I _____ in English and in
Spanish.

Thanks for your letter! And thanks to your
grandmother, too!

Enrique

B Write *Do you* questions. Use part A to help you. Then write short answers using your own information.

1. (live / Spain)

   Q: _Do you live in Spain?_____ **A:** _Yes, I do._ OR _No, I don't._

2. (listen / CDs)

   Q: _____ **A:** _____

3. (have / brothers and sisters)

   Q: _____ **A:** _____

4. (sing / songs in English)

   Q: _____ **A:** _____

C Read about Roger. Then correct the sentences.

I'm Roger Leconte. I live in Montreal, Canada, with my parents and my little sister, Nicole. I go to a small school in the city. My first language is French, but I speak English, too. In my free time, I play video games and listen to music. I don't like rap music very much, but I love rock. On weekends, I hang out at the park with my friends, but I eat with my family.

1. Roger lives in the United States.

   Roger doesn't live in the United States. He lives in Canada.

2. He has a little brother.

   _____

3. He speaks Spanish and Portuguese.

   _____

4. Roger plays soccer and watches TV.

   _____

5. He likes rap music.

   _____

6. He hangs out at the mall on weekends.

   _____

Sports fun

1. Vocabulary

🔊 **A** Who does these sports, Claudia or Zach? Listen and write
C (Claudia) or Z (Zach).

I surf. _____

I do karate. __C__

I skateboard. _____

I go biking. _____

I water-ski. _____

I play baseball. _____

I swim. _____

I ski. _____

🔊 **B** Listen and practice.

C What sports do you do? What sports don't you do? Write sentences.

Sports I do	Sports I don't do
I skateboard.	*I don't ski.*

2. Language focus

Does he / she . . . ?

Does he do karate?
Yes, he does.
No, he doesn't.

A Claudia and Zach talk about a new student. Listen and practice.

Claudia Hey, that guy's new. Who is he?
Zach That's Chris.
Claudia Does he like sports?
Zach Well, . . .
Claudia Does he do karate?
Zach No, he doesn't.
Claudia Does he play baseball?
Zach No, he doesn't.
Claudia Does he surf?
Zach Uh . . . yes, he does. He surfs the Internet!

B Chris and Zach talk about Claudia. Complete the conversation. Listen and check. Then practice.

Chris Wow! Your friend Claudia is good at basketball.
_____Does_____ she play other sports?
Zach _____, she does. She's very athletic.
Chris _____ she play soccer?
Zach Yes, she _____. She likes it very much.
Chris _____ she have a gym partner?
Zach No, she _____.
Chris Hey, maybe she can be my partner!
She can help me!

3. Pronunciation Intonation

Listen. Notice the rising intonation in *Yes / No* questions. Then listen again and practice.

Does he swim? Does he surf? Does she do karate? Does she play soccer?

4. Speaking

Play a game. Think of a sports star. Give clues. Your classmates guess.

You He's a sports star.	**Classmate 3** Is he American?
Classmate 1 Does he ski?	**You** Yes, he is.
You No, he doesn't.	**Classmate 4** Is he Andre Agassi?
Classmate 2 Does he play tennis?	**You** Yes, he is!
You Yes, he does.	

Sports and Activities 31

Lesson 12 · Sports equipment

1. Vocabulary

◁)) **A** Where does Claudia wear this sports equipment? Write the correct word next to each body part. Then listen and practice.

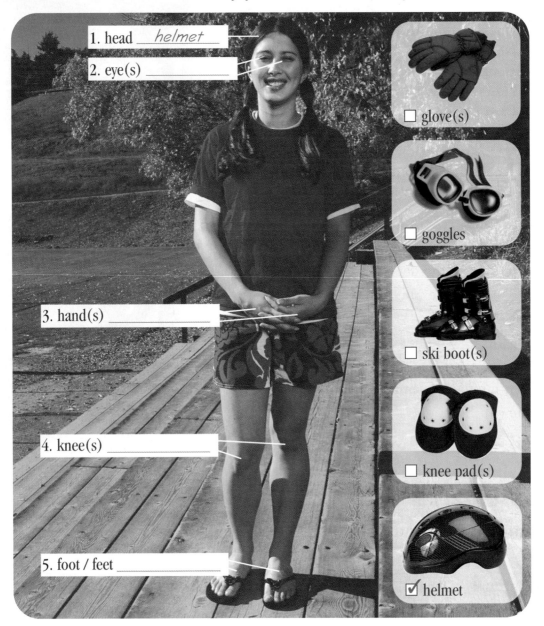

1. head _helmet_
2. eye(s) _____

3. hand(s) _____

4. knee(s) _____

5. foot / feet _____

☐ glove(s)

☐ goggles

☐ ski boot(s)

☐ knee pad(s)

☑ helmet

B What sports equipment do these athletes wear? Make guesses and complete the chart.

a skateboarder	a skier	a cyclist
helmet		

32   Unit 3

2. Language focus

A Claudia's little brother, Oscar, helps get the sports equipment. Listen and practice.

They + verb: statements	
They wear goggles.	
They don't wear helmets.	
Do they + verb: questions	
Do they wear gloves?	
Yes, they do.	
No, they don't.	

Claudia Oscar, can you help me, please? I need the sports equipment for the swim team.

Oscar Sure! Here is the helmet . . .

Claudia Huh? Swimmers don't wear helmets.

Oscar Um, do they wear gloves?

Claudia No, they don't. They wear goggles.

Oscar Oh! Um, do swimmers wear knee pads?

Claudia No, they don't. They don't wear knee pads!

Oscar Sorry. I don't know a lot about sports.

Claudia No kidding!

B How much do you know about sports? Answer the questions. Listen and check. Then practice.

1. **Q:** Do skiers wear sneakers?

   A: *No, they don't.*

2. **Q:** Do soccer players have uniforms?

   A: _____

3. **Q:** Do baseball players play on a court?

   A: _____

4. **Q:** Do cyclists wear hats?

   A: _____

5. **Q:** Do skateboarders use knee pads?

   A: _____

6. **Q:** Do basketball players play on a field?

   A: _____

3. Listening

Claudia plays a game with Oscar. What athletes do they talk about? Listen and number the pictures.

Sports and Activities 33

Mini-review

1. Language check

Complete the interview with Jane Cook, a champion skateboarder.
Use *do*, *does*, *don't*, and *doesn't*.

SPORTS FOR KIDS

Interviewer Hi, Jane. Nice to meet you.
Jane Hi!
Interviewer Jane, we know you love sports. Do your parents like sports, too?
Jane Yes, they ___do___ My dad likes outdoor sports.
Interviewer _____ he go biking?
Jane Yes, he _____. He goes biking every day, actually.
Interviewer And your mother? _____ she go biking, too?
Jane No, she _____. She swims and water-skis.
Interviewer And your sisters? _____ they skateboard?
Jane No, they _____. They like team sports, like soccer and basketball.
Interviewer What about you? _____ you play team sports?
Jane No, I _____. I skateboard, of course. And I run every day, too.

**Champion Skateboarder
Jane Cook, 12 – Miami, Florida**

2. Listening

A Listen to more of the interviewer's questions. Check (✓) the correct responses.

1. ☑ No, they don't. They don't like water sports.
   ☐ Yes, they do. They play every weekend.

2. ☐ Yes, I do. It's fun.
   ☐ Yes, they do. They love the mountains.

3. ☐ No, it isn't.
   ☐ Yes, he does. He's a great player.

4. ☐ Yes, she does. She's on the team.
   ☐ Yes, she is. She likes karate.

5. ☐ Yes, we do. Every summer.
   ☐ No, he doesn't. He doesn't like the water.

B Now listen to the complete interview in part A. Check your answers.

3. Game Play Ball!

A Work with a classmate. Read the clues. Then write the correct words on the ball. The pair that finishes first is the winner.

a. A biker wears a 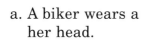 on his or her head.

b. A lot of people do in Asia.

c. Skateboarders wear knee .

d. Tennis players wear on their feet.

e. People at the beach.

f. You can in a park.

g. A baseball player has a .

h. Each player wears a with a number.

i. is a fun sport.

j. Teams play on a field.

k. People in a pool or at the beach.

l. People wear gloves on their 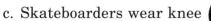.

B Write each numbered letter from the puzzle in the correct place. Then write the answer.

Q: ___ _h_ ___ ___ ___ ___ ___ ___ ___ ___
    1   2   3   4   5   6   7   8   9   10

  ___ ___ ___ ___ ___ ___ _t_ ___ ___ ___ ___ ___ ___?
  11 12 13 14 15 16 17 18   19 20 21 22 23

A: _____

Lesson 13 Off to camp

1. Vocabulary

🔊 **A** Megan packs to go to camp. Read the checklist. Label the pictures. Then listen and practice.

Camp Coby Camper Checklist
Bring:
- ☐ blanket
- ☑ bug repellent
- ☐ flashlight
- ☐ hiking boots
- ☐ pillow
- ☐ raincoat
- ☐ sleeping bag
- ☐ soap
- ☐ sunscreen
- ☐ towel

Remember:
No cell phones
No computers
No radios
No video games

1. *bug repellent*
2. _____
3. _____
4. _____
5. _____
6. _____
7. _____
8. _____
9. _____
10. _____

B Complete the sentences with the words in part A.

1. The *bug repellent* is on the desk.
2. The _____ is under the desk.
3. The _____ is on the desk.
4. The _____ is on top of the blanket.
5. The _____ is next to the bed.
6. The _____ is on the bed.
7. The _____ is under the bed.
8. The _____ is under the chair.
9. The _____ is on the chair.
10. The _____ are next to the desk.

2. Language focus

A Megan's mother helps Megan pack for camp. Listen and practice.

Megan	Let's go. Hurry up, Mom.
Mom	Just a minute, Megan. Don't wear a dress. Wear something comfortable.
Megan	But this *is* comfortable, Mom.
Mom	Fine, Megan, but read the checklist again. It says "No computers." Leave your computer at home, please.
Megan	But I use my computer at night, Mom.
Mom	I know, but there are camp activities at night.
Megan	Oh, good! I can stay up until midnight.
Mom	No, Megan! It's camp. Don't stay up late.
Megan	Mom, please stop. Camp is supposed to be fun!

Imperatives

Hurry up.
Don't stay up late.

B Look at the checklist in 1A. Can you guess the Camp Coby rules? Complete the rules. Then listen and check.

Camp Coby Rules

1. *Don't play* video games. (play / don't play)
2. _____ hiking boots. (wear / don't wear)
3. _____ to the radio. (listen / don't listen)
4. _____ cell phones. (bring / don't bring)
5. _____ computers. (use / don't use)
6. _____ a flashlight. (bring / don't bring)
7. _____ sunscreen. (use / don't use)

3. Speaking

Write four crazy rules for Camp Coby. Close your book and tell your rules to your classmates. Who has the craziest rules?

Get up at 11:00 every day.

1.
2.
3.
4.

Sports and Activities   37

1. Vocabulary

🔊 **A** Look at the Camp Coby Web site. Match the photos to the correct activities. Then listen and practice.

Campers . . .

☐ cook hot dogs.	☐ go canoeing.	☐ go hiking.	☐ take swimming lessons.
1 do arts and crafts.	☐ go horseback riding.	☐ make a campfire.	☐ tell stories.

🔊 **B** What do campers do at Camp Coby? Listen and write an activity for each time.

8:00 A.M.	*They go horseback riding.*
10:00 A.M.	
1:15 P.M.	
3:30 P.M.	
4:45 P.M.	
8:15 P.M.	
8:30 P.M.	
9:00 P.M.	

2. Language focus

🔊 **A** Megan's parents read her letter. Listen and practice.

Mom Wow! Megan is very busy at Camp Coby!

Dad Great! What time does she get up?

Mom She gets up at 6:30.

Dad Wow. Campers get up early. What do they do every day?

Mom Let's see. They do arts and crafts, they go canoeing, they go hiking, . . .

Dad When do they go hiking?

Mom They go hiking in the afternoon.

Dad It sounds like fun! Can parents go to camp, too?

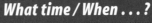

What time / When . . . ?
What time does Megan get up?
She gets up **at 6:30**.
At 6:30.
When do they go hiking?
They go hiking **in the afternoon**.
They go hiking **at 2:00**.
At 2:00.

in the morning = *about 5 A.M. to 12 P.M.*
in the afternoon = *about 12 P.M. to 6 P.M.*
in the evening = *about 6 P.M. to 10 P.M.*
at night = *about 10 P.M. to 5 A.M.*

🔊 **B** Look at the schedule in 1B. Write questions about Megan. Use *When* or *What time*. Listen and check. Then practice.

1. **Q:** _When does Megan take swimming lessons?_ OR
   What time does Megan take swimming lessons?
   A: She takes swimming lessons at 10:00.

2. **Q:** _____
   A: She goes canoeing in the afternoon.

3. **Q:** _____
   A: At 4:45.

4. **Q:** _____
   A: At 8:15.

5. **Q:** _____
   A: She tells stories in the evening.

3. Listening

🔊 Listen to the activities at another camp – Camp Oakley. When do campers do these activities? Check (✓) the correct times of the day.

	in the morning	in the afternoon	in the evening	at night
1. go hiking	✓	☐	☐	☐
2. go horseback riding	☐	☐	☐	☐
3. do arts and crafts	☐	☐	☐	☐
4. take swimming lessons	☐	☐	☐	☐
5. tell stories	☐	☐	☐	☐

Connections

1. Reading

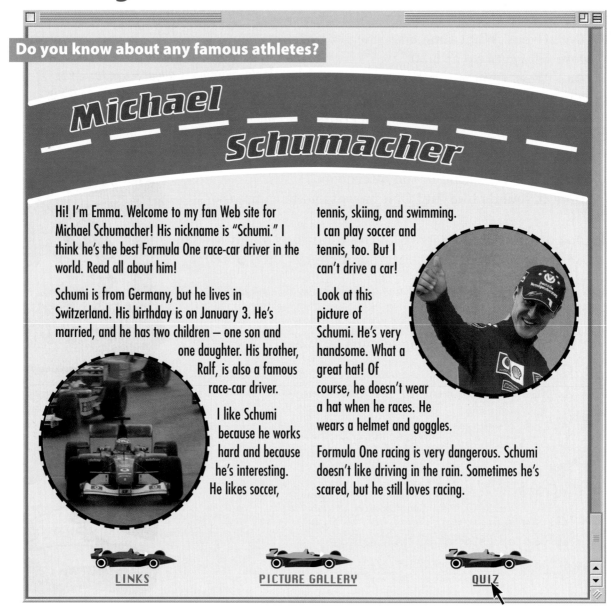

Do you know about any famous athletes?

Michael Schumacher

Hi! I'm Emma. Welcome to my fan Web site for Michael Schumacher! His nickname is "Schumi." I think he's the best Formula One race-car driver in the world. Read all about him!

Schumi is from Germany, but he lives in Switzerland. His birthday is on January 3. He's married, and he has two children — one son and one daughter. His brother, Ralf, is also a famous race-car driver.

I like Schumi because he works hard and because he's interesting. He likes soccer, tennis, skiing, and swimming. I can play soccer and tennis, too. But I can't drive a car!

Look at this picture of Schumi. He's very handsome. What a great hat! Of course, he doesn't wear a hat when he races. He wears a helmet and goggles.

Formula One racing is very dangerous. Schumi doesn't like driving in the rain. Sometimes he's scared, but he still loves racing.

LINKS   PICTURE GALLERY   QUIZ

A Read the fan Web site for Michael Schumacher.

B Take Emma's quiz about Michael Schumacher. Write the answers.

1. Where's Michael Schumacher from?
   He's from ____Germany____ .

2. What's his nickname?
   It's _____ .

3. When's his birthday?
   It's _____ .

4. Does he have children?
   _____

5. Can his brother drive a car?
   _____

6. Does Michael Schumacher wear a hat when he races?
   _____

2. Listening

🔊 **A** Erica and Joe play a game. Joe tries to guess the name of a famous athlete. Listen and check (✓) T (true) or F (false).

	T	F
1. He plays on a team.	☐	☑
2. He plays outside.	☐	☐
3. He doesn't play on a field.	☐	☐
4. He wears a uniform.	☐	☐
5. He doesn't wear ski boots.	☐	☐
6. He's from Argentina.	☐	☐

B Write the type of sport and the athlete's name.

Sport: _____   Athlete: _____

3. Writing

Read about Gustavo Kuerten. Then write a Web site article about Gustavo or your favorite athlete. Use the information about Gustavo Kuerten or your own ideas.

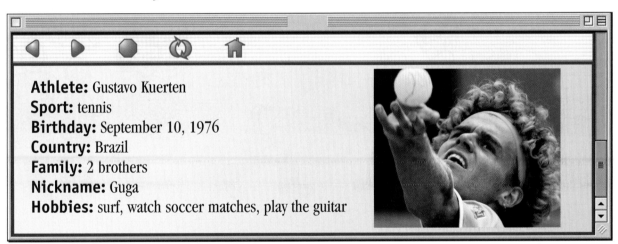

Athlete: Gustavo Kuerten
Sport: tennis
Birthday: September 10, 1976
Country: Brazil
Family: 2 brothers
Nickname: Guga
Hobbies: surf, watch soccer matches, play the guitar

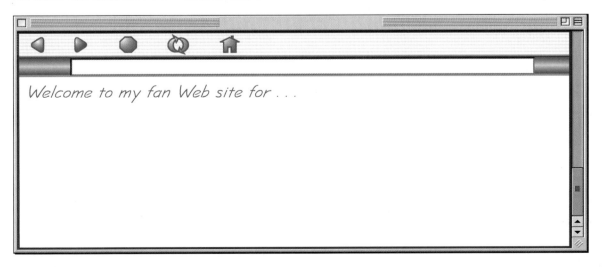

Welcome to my fan Web site for . . .

Lessons 11-15 Review

Language chart review

Simple present		
They + verb: statements	**Yes/No questions: he/she/they**	**Short answers**
Skateboarders wear helmets. **They don't wear** goggles.	**Does he swim?**	Yes, he does. No, he doesn't.
	Does she do karate?	Yes, she does. No, she doesn't.
	Do they like sports?	Yes, they do. No, they don't.

A The basketball team at Ryder School is very unusual. Look at the picture. Write *Do* or *Does* questions about the team. Use the correct forms of the verbs. Then answer the questions.

1. the players / play in the gym

   Q: _Do the players play in the gym?_   **A:** _No, they don't. They play in the cafeteria._

2. the players / wear sneakers

   Q: _____   **A:** _____

3. the coach / wear goggles

   Q: _____   **A:** _____

4. player 2 / have a basketball

   Q: _____   **A:** _____

5. players 4 and 5 / listen to music

   Q: _____   **A:** _____

Language chart review

Imperatives	What time . . . ?	When . . . ?
Read a book. **Don't play video games.**	**What time** does he go hiking? He goes hiking **at 5:00**. **At 5:00.**	**When** do they use their computers? They use their computers **at night**. They use their computers **at 7:30**. **At 7:30.**

B Write imperatives with the verb phrases in the box.

☐ go to bed early   ☐ swim there   ☑ talk on your cell phone   ☐ use sunscreen

1. *Don't talk on your cell phone.*   2. _____

3. _____   4. _____

C Two swimming coaches are talking about their teams. Complete
the conversation with the sentences in the box.

☐ a. What time do they eat breakfast?   ☑ d. Does Maggie Ferre swim on your team?
☐ b. So, when do your swimmers practice?   ☐ e. What about her brother, Joe? Does he swim, too?
☐ c. What time do they swim?

Coach Sala ___d___
Coach Hanes Yes, she does.
Coach Sala _____
Coach Hanes No, he doesn't. He's on the baseball team.
Coach Sala _____

Coach Hanes They practice in the morning.
Coach Sala _____
Coach Hanes Very early. At 6:30.
Coach Sala _____
Coach Hanes After they practice. At 8:00.

16 I like music.

1. Vocabulary ....•

◁)) **A** Listen to these kinds of music and practice.

classical country hip-hop jazz pop reggae rock

◁)) **B** Work with your classmates. Look at the photos, and complete
the labels with words from part A. Then listen and practice.

My Interests

Unit 4

🎵 **Music Magazine**
Top Musicians of the Year

Pink

LL Cool J

Shaggy

Yo-Yo Ma

1. *classical* musician

2. _____ singer

3. _____ singer

4. _____ singer

Lenny Kravitz

The Dixie Chicks

Wynton Marsalis

5. _____ singer

6. _____ group

7. _____ musician

C Play a chain game. Learn the kinds of music your classmates like.

Camilo What's your favorite kind of music, Yumi?
Yumi My favorite kind of music is jazz.

⌐→ **Yumi** What's your favorite kind of music, Leah?
Leah My favorite kind of music is pop.

⌐→ **Leah** What's your favorite kind of music, . . . ?

2. Language focus

her / him / it / them
She's great. I like **her** a lot. He's my favorite. I like **him** a lot.
Hip-hop is cool. I like **it**. They're boring. I don't like **them** at all.

🔊 **A** Daisy Fines of *Music Magazine* interviews Ana. Listen and practice.

Daisy So, Ana, what's your favorite kind of music?

Ana Well, I think country is cool. The Dixie Chicks are great. I really like them.

Daisy I do, too! They're a *great* country group! How about other kinds of music? Do you like jazz?

Ana No, I don't like it at all.

Daisy Really? What about Wynton Marsalis? A lot of people like him.

Ana Well, yeah, I guess he's OK. But I don't listen to much jazz. I like country, pop, and rock.

Daisy Do you listen to Pink?

Ana Yes! I love her! She's my favorite pop singer.

🔊 **B** What do other teens tell Daisy? Complete their sentences with *her*, *him*, *it*, or *them*. Then listen and check.

1. Pop music isn't interesting. I don't like ____*it*____ .
2. The Dixie Chicks are boring. I don't like _____ at all.
3. Alan Jackson is my favorite country singer. I love _____ .
4. Classical is my favorite kind of music. I like _____ a lot.
5. Pink is weird. I don't like _____ .
6. Shaggy is great. I love _____ .

3. Speaking

Complete questions 6, 7, and 8. Then ask a classmate the questions.

Do you like . . . ?	a lot	a little	not at all
1. jazz	☐	☐	☐
2. country	☐	☐	☐
3. rock	☐	☐	☐
4. hip-hop	☐	☐	☐
5. reggae	☐	☐	☐
6. _____ (male singer)	☐	☐	☐
7. _____ (female singer)	☐	☐	☐
8. _____ (group)	☐	☐	☐

Peter, do you like jazz?

No, I don't like it at all.

Lesson 17 Let's look online.

1. Prices

🔊 Study the prices. Then listen and practice.

1. $16.00 = sixteen dollars
2. $24.50 = twenty-four fifty OR twenty-four dollars and fifty cents
3. $58.97 = fifty-eight ninety-seven OR fifty-eight dollars and ninety-seven cents
4. $19.04 = nineteen-oh-four OR nineteen dollars and four cents

2. Vocabulary

🔊 **A** Look at some items in the *Discover Your World* online catalog.
Listen and practice.

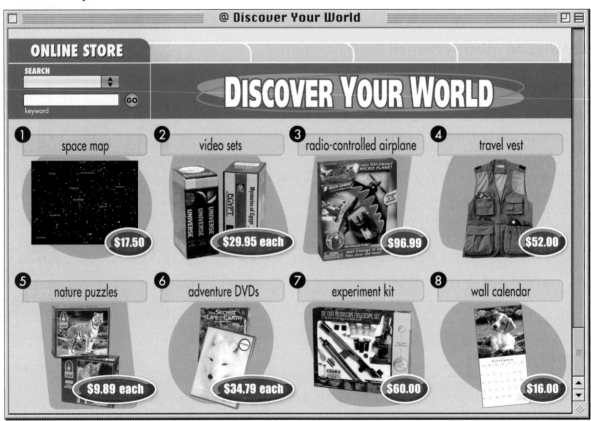

🔊 **B** Look at the items and prices in part A. Listen and practice.

C Practice saying the items and prices with a classmate.

> The travel vest.

> The nature puzzles.

> The travel vest is fifty-two dollars.

> The nature puzzles are nine ninety-eight each.

3. Language focus

A Tommy talks to Kate about things in the online catalog. Listen and practice.

How much is / are . . . ?
How much is it?
It's **$96.99**.
How much are the video sets?
They**'re $29.99** each.

Tommy Hey! This is a great Web site!
All these things are cool. There's a great radio-controlled airplane.
Kate Really? Radio-controlled? How much is it?
Tommy It's $96.99.
Kate That's almost a hundred dollars!
Tommy I know. I like these video sets, too.
Kate How much are they?
Tommy They're $29.99 each.
Kate Hmm. That's expensive.

B Complete the rest of the conversation. Listen and check. Then practice.

Tommy Wow! I like these nature puzzles.
Kate *How much are* _____ they?
Tommy _____ $9.89 each.
And there are some interesting adventure DVDs.
Kate _____
the DVDs?
Tommy _____ $34.79 each.
And this experiment kit is nice.
Kate And _____
the experiment kit, Tommy?
Tommy Oh. _____ $60.00.
Kate You like a lot of things, Tommy. Too bad you don't have a lot of money!

4. Listening

Tommy and Kate compare prices in their catalogs. Listen and write the prices in the chart.

	watch	nature puzzles	camera	hiking boots	backpack
Tommy's online catalog	$39.99				
Kate's catalog	$29.99				

Mini-review

1. Language check

A Ryan and Ashley shop for a birthday present for their friend, Matt. Complete the conversation with the correct words. Then practice.

Ryan It's Matt's birthday on Sunday. What can we get _him_ (her / him)?

Ashley How about a CD? Does he like reggae?

Ryan No, he doesn't like _____ (it / them) at all.

Ashley Well, what about pop? Does he like pop?

Ryan Yes. Actually, he loves _____ (it / them). His favorite singer is Pink.

Ashley Really? I like _____ (him / her), too.

Ryan Oh, look. Here's a CD by the Dixie Chicks.

Ashley Does Matt like the Dixie Chicks?

Ryan Yes, he loves _____ (it / them).

Ashley Great. How much _____ (is / are) the CD?

Ryan _____ (It's / They're) $13.95.

Ashley OK. Let's buy _____ (it / them).

B Ryan asks Ashley about the prices of other things in the music store. Write their questions and answers.

video $19.99

DVDs $32.99

T-shirt $8.99

posters $5.99 each

1. **Ryan** _How much is the video?_

   Ashley _It's nineteen ninety-nine._ OR _It's nineteen dollars and ninety-nine cents._

2. **Ryan** _____

   Ashley _____

3. **Ryan** _____

   Ashley _____

4. **Ryan** _____

   Ashley _____

2. Game All About Music

Play the game with a classmate. Use things in your bag as game markers. Take turns.

- Close your eyes and touch one of the numbers.
- Move your marker that number of spaces.
- Complete the sentence or follow the directions.

START

3/4

I think country music is _____ .

A music CD costs _____ .

You win a music contest!
Take another turn.

The name of a hip-hop singer is _____ .

Five kinds of music are _____ .

Ask a classmate a question.

My favorite singer or group is _____ .

A rock band I like is _____ .

Ask a classmate a question.

My classmate's favorite singer or group is _____ . (Ask him or her.)

_____ is my favorite kind of music. I like it a lot.

You are very musical.
Take another turn.

You are late for music class. Lose a turn.

I think _____ music is boring. I don't like it at all.

FINISH

A rock group I don't like is _____ .

My mother's or father's favorite kind of music is _____ .

Tell a classmate two groups you like.

A famous singer, musician, or group from my country is _____ .

Our interests

1. Vocabulary

◁)) **A** These students sign up for a summer exchange program. Read about their free-time activities. Then listen and practice.

José I go camping.

Diana I write poetry.

Carla I go dancing a lot.

Ted I spend time at the beach.

Joleen I go shopping with my friends.

Jill I do crossword puzzles.

B Match two students in part A to the host student below with similar interests. Write their names.

I love the outdoors. I'm a very active person.

Tiago, Brazil

_____

_____

I stay home a lot. I like quiet activities.

Gina, Canada

_____

_____

I go out, and I do a lot of things with my friends.

Luz, Puerto Rico

_____

_____

C You want to be a host student. How do you describe yourself? Tell your classmates. Use words from part A or your own ideas.

I like sports. I play tennis a lot. I spend time with my friends. I . . .

2. Language focus

> **like / don't like + to (verb)**
>
> I **like to go** shopping.
> I **like to play** video games.
> I **don't like to practice** the piano.

A Eliana applies to an exchange program. Read her application form. Then listen and practice.

> 1. Name: *Eliana da Costa*   2. Age: *16*
> 3. Country: *Brazil*
> 4. Activities you like to do / don't like to do:
>   *I like to go swimming. I also like to go*
>   *shopping. I don't like to watch TV.*
> 5. Do you like to go camping? *No, I don't.*
> 6. Do you like to spend time at home?
>   *Yes, I do.*

B Complete the form with your own information.

> 1. Name: _____   2. Age: _____
> 3. Country: _____
> 4. Activities you like to do / don't like to do:
>   _____
>   _____
> 5. Do you like to go camping? _____
> 6. Do you like to spend time at home?
>   _____

C Tell your classmates things you like and don't like to do. Use 1A or your own information.

> I like to listen to music. I don't like to go camping. I . . .

3. Listening

An exchange student, Carla, is staying with Luz's family. Luz is talking to her friend, Eva, about the experience. Who likes to do these activities? Listen and check (✓) the correct boxes.

	Carla	Luz	Carla and Luz
1. go dancing	☐	☐	☐
2. go shopping	☐	☐	☐
3. play tennis	☐	☐	☐
4. go to the movies	☐	☐	☐

Lesson 19 In and out of school

1. Language focus

A Take the survey. Circle a letter to complete each sentence.

Adverbs of frequency	
100%	I **always** do my homework.
	I **usually** come to class on time.
	Sometimes I talk in class.
	I **sometimes** talk in class.
	I **hardly ever** sleep in class.
0%	I **never** throw paper airplanes.

SURVEY
What Kind of Student Are You?

1. I _____ do my homework.
   a. always
   b. usually
   c. sometimes
   d. hardly ever
   e. never

2. I _____ come to class on time.
   a. always
   b. usually
   c. sometimes
   d. hardly ever
   e. never

3. I _____ listen to the teacher.
   a. always
   b. usually
   c. sometimes
   d. hardly ever
   e. never

4. I _____ answer a lot of the teacher's questions.
   a. always
   b. usually
   c. sometimes
   d. hardly ever
   e. never

5. I _____ listen to music on my headphones in class.
   a. always
   b. usually
   c. sometimes
   d. hardly ever
   e. never

6. I _____ get good grades.
   a. always
   b. usually
   c. sometimes
   d. hardly ever
   e. never

7. I _____ sleep in class.
   a. always
   b. usually
   c. sometimes
   d. hardly ever
   e. never

8. I _____ throw paper airplanes in class.
   a. always
   b. usually
   c. sometimes
   d. hardly ever
   e. never

B Zach completes the survey in part A. Listen and write his answers on the lines. Then practice.

C Play a chain game. Find out your classmates' responses to the survey items.

Mario I always do my homework. How about you, Yumi?

Yumi I usually do my homework.

> **Yumi** I hardly ever get good grades. How about you, Leah?

Leah Sometimes I get good grades.

> **Leah** I never sleep in class. How about you, . . . ?

52 Unit 4

2. Listening

🔊 **A** Ana talks about her weekend activities. How often does she do these things? Listen and write *A* for Ana in the correct columns.

Weekend activities	always	usually	sometimes	hardly ever	never
1. go dancing			*A*		
2. go shopping					
3. sleep late					
4. read books					
5. go bowling					

🔊 **B** How often does Charlie do the things in part A? Listen again and write *C* for Charlie in the correct columns in part A.

3. Speaking

A What do you do after school? Write sentences. Use the activities in the box or your own ideas.

☐ do my homework   ☐ go shopping   ☐ play the guitar   ☐ use the Internet   ☐ watch TV

(always) *I always watch TV after school.*

1. (always) _____

2. (usually) _____

3. (sometimes) _____

4. (hardly ever) _____

5. (never) _____

B Work with a classmate. Read your sentences from part A to each other. Then tell the class two things about your classmate.

> Nadia always goes to soccer practice after school. She hardly ever goes shopping.

Connections

1. Reading

What do teens in your country like to do in their free time? What do you like to do?

American Teens and Free Time

American teens are busy. So in their free time, they like to relax and have fun.

Teens like to watch TV. They watch it 11.3 hours a week. And music? Teens love it! They listen to tapes and CDs 9.9 hours a week. And they listen to the radio 10.3 hours a week.

Of course, teens like to spend time with their friends. They hang out with friends 9.1 hours a week. Sometimes they go shopping. Teens don't think malls are boring. They like them a lot! On average, teens spend 3.2 hours a week at malls.

Teens like to chat online. But many teens like to talk on the phone, too. They talk on the phone 6.4 hours a week.

Teens like to do many other things. But they watch TV, listen to music, hang out, and talk – a lot! American teens have fun, but they're not always active!

Source: *Kidbits*.

A Read the article about how American teens spend their free time.

B Write the correct activity from the box on each bar of the graph. Use the information in part A.

> ☐ hang out at malls ☐ listen to tapes and CDs ☐ talk on the phone
> ☐ hang out with friends ☐ listen to the radio ☑ watch TV

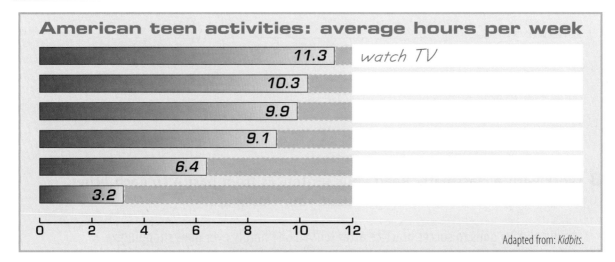

American teen activities: average hours per week

	Hours	Activity
	11.3	*watch TV*
	10.3	
	9.9	
	9.1	
	6.4	
	3.2	

Adapted from: *Kidbits*.

2. Listening

A Look at Steven's room. Guess which statements are true or false for him. Check (✓) T (true) or F (false).

	My guess T	My guess F	Correct information T	Correct information F
1. I always hang out in my room after school.	☐	☐	☐	☐
2. I never eat in my room.	☐	☐	☐	☐
3. My room is messy, but I love it.	☐	☐	☐	☐
4. I like to play sports.	☐	☐	☐	☐
5. I always watch TV in my room.	☐	☐	☐	☐
6. I read comic books.	☐	☐	☐	☐
7. I usually listen to classical music. I like it a lot.	☐	☐	☐	☐
8. I hardly ever listen to rock.	☐	☐	☐	☐
9. I collect posters of my favorite athletes.	☐	☐	☐	☐
10. I take guitar lessons.	☐	☐	☐	☐

B Now listen to Steven, and check (✓) the correct information.

3. Writing

A Write five things you like to do and the average number of hours per week you do them.

go shopping   3.5 hours
1.
2.
3.
4.
5.

B Write an article about the things you do every week. Use the information from part A and the reading in 1A to help you.

I _____ about _____ hours a week. I . . .

Review

Lessons 16–20

Language chart review

her / him / it / them	like / don't like + to (verb)
She's cool. I like **her**.	I **like to hang out** with friends.
He's a pop singer. I like **him** a lot.	I **don't like to stay** home.
Jazz is boring. I don't like **it**.	
These CDs are great. I like **them**.	

A Read these sentences. Then write sentences with *like* or *don't like*.

1. My new neighbors are great!
   I like them.

2. That book is boring.
   _____

3. She's my best friend.
   _____

4. My baby brother is really cute.
   _____

5. Snakes are dangerous.
   _____

6. I think rock is cool.
   _____

B Josh writes an e-mail message to you. Read Josh's message. Then complete your message to him. Tell him about your free-time activities. Use *like to* and *don't like to*.

Hi!

My name's Josh. Here are some of the things I like to do: listen to music, go camping, spend time with my family, and play the piano.

But I don't dance. I don't play basketball or soccer. I'm musical, but I'm not athletic! How about you? What are your interests?

Your friend,

Josh

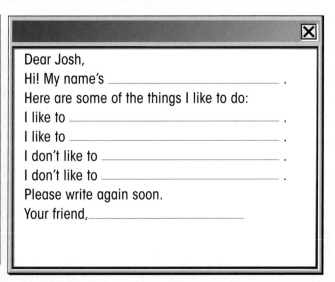

Dear Josh,
Hi! My name's _____.
Here are some of the things I like to do:
I like to _____.
I like to _____.
I don't like to _____.
I don't like to _____.
Please write again soon.
Your friend,_____

56 Unit 4

Language chart review

How much is / are . . . ?	Adverbs of frequency
How much is this DVD? It's **$29.99**. **How much are** those boots? They**'re $60.00**.	100% **I always** get good grades. **I usually** get up early. **Sometimes I / I sometimes** hang out with friends. **I hardly ever** go to bed early. 0% **I never** stay home on Friday night.

C Complete the questions with *How much is* or *How much are*. Then look at the photos, and answer the questions.

 $6.95 each  $9.79 each  $89.00  $49.95

1. **Q:** _How much are_____ those puzzles? **A:** _They're six ninety-five each._

2. **Q:** _____ the skateboard? **A:** _____

3. **Q:** _____ that experiment kit? **A:** _____

4. **Q:** _____ those cameras? **A:** _____

D How often does Sam do these things? Look at his schedule. Then write sentences with *always, usually, sometimes, hardly ever,* or *never*.

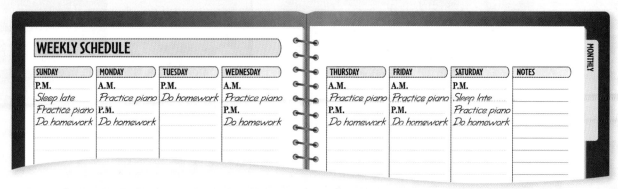

1. (do homework at night)

   I always do my homework at night.

2. (sleep late)

   _____

3. (practice the piano in the morning)

   _____

4. (practice the piano in the afternoon)

   _____

5. (go bowling)

In San Francisco

1. Vocabulary

◁» **A** Claudia and her family are on vacation in San Francisco.
What do they do there? Match the photos to the correct activities.
Then listen and practice.

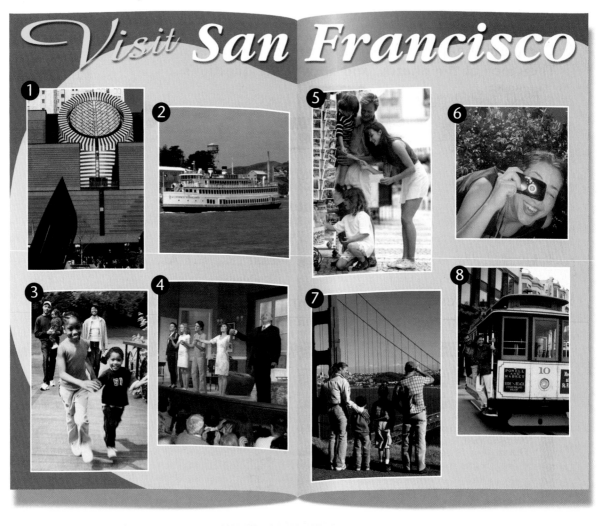

In San Francisco, they . . .

☐ buy souvenirs.	☐ ride a trolley.	☐ take a boat ride.	*1* visit a museum.
☐ go sightseeing.	☐ see a show.	☐ take pictures.	☐ walk in the park.

B Write things people can do in your town or city.
Use part A to help you or your own ideas.

1. *Take a boat ride.* _____   4. _____

2. _____   5. _____

3. _____   6. _____

2. Language focus

◁)) A Claudia is videotaping her trip to San Francisco. Listen and practice.

Today is our first day in San Francisco. I'm videotaping our trip. Right now, we're visiting Fisherman's Wharf. Let's see. . . . There are Mom and Dad. They're buying souvenirs. My cousin, Ruben, is eating lunch over there. My brother, Oscar, is taking pictures with his new camera. And now you see me. You can do so much in San Francisco. It's a great city!

Present continuous affirmative statements
I**'m videotaping** our trip.
She**'s taking** pictures.
We**'re visiting** Fisherman's Wharf.
You**'re skateboarding**.
They**'re buying** souvenirs.
buying = buy + ing
taking = take̸ + ing

◁)) B Everybody is doing different things now. Write the sentences with the correct forms of the verbs. Listen and check.

1. (Ruben / go sightseeing) *He's going sightseeing.*

2. (Mom and Dad / see a show) _____

3. (Oscar / take pictures) _____

4. (Oscar and I / take a boat ride) _____

3. Speaking

Imagine you are on vacation. Think of an activity. Act it out. Your classmates guess.

Classmate 1	You're skateboarding.
You	No, I'm not.
Classmate 2	You're in-line skating.
You	That's right! I'm in-line skating.

Lesson 22 At the park

1. Vocabulary

A Ms. Day and Mr. Green take their students to the park. Match the rules in the box to the correct signs in the picture. Then listen and practice.

> **1** Eat in the picnic area. **3** Stand in line. **5** Throw trash in the trash can.
> **2** Sit down in the boat. **4** Stay on the bike path. **6** Wait for the green light.

B Look at part A again. Read the sentences and check (✓) T (true) or F (false).

			T	F
1.		They're waiting for the green light.	✓	☐
2.		Mariah and Nathan are staying on the bike path.	☐	☐
3.		The girls are eating in the picnic area.	☐	☐
4.		Joe is standing in line.	☐	☐
5.		He's throwing trash in the trash can.	☐	☐

2. Language focus

🔊 **A** The students aren't following the rules. Listen and practice.

Present continuous negative statements	

I**'m not paying** attention.
You **aren't standing** in line.
He **isn't standing** in line.
We **aren't following** the rules.
They **aren't staying** on the bike path.

aren't = are not   isn't = is not

Ms. Day Oh, no. The students aren't following the rules! Look at Joe. He isn't standing in line.

Mr. Green Hey, Joe! You aren't standing in line!

Ms. Day And look at Nathan and Mariah. They aren't staying on the bike path.

Mr. Green Nathan! Mariah! Please stay on the bike path.

Ms. Day Oh, no, wait! It's a red light. I'm not paying attention.

Mr. Green You're right. Now *we* aren't following the rules!

🔊 **B** Look at the picture in 1A again. What are the students doing wrong? Complete the sentences. Then listen and check.

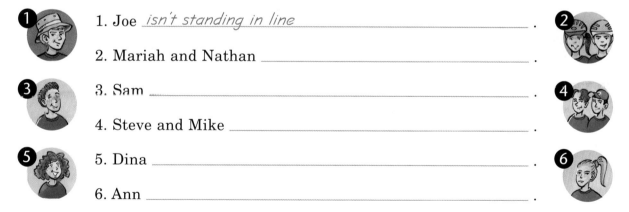

1. Joe *isn't standing in line* .

2. Mariah and Nathan _____ .

3. Sam _____ .

4. Steve and Mike _____ .

5. Dina _____ .

6. Ann _____ .

3. Listening

🔊 Now what are the students doing wrong? Listen and match the two parts of each sentence.

1. Ann and Dina aren't *b*   a. sitting down in the boat.
2. Mike isn't _____   b. eating in the picnic area.
3. Joe and Sam aren't _____   c. standing in line.
4. Steve isn't _____   d. staying on the bike path.
5. Mariah isn't _____   e. throwing trash in the trash can.

Mini-review

1. Language check

Look at the photos. What is everyone doing? Correct the sentences.

7:00 A.M.

1. Kate's reading a book. _She isn't reading a book. She's doing her homework._

2. Rafael's taking a boat ride. _____

3. Claudia's visiting a museum. _____

4. Zach's watching a video. _____

7:00 P.M.

5. Rafael's walking in the park. _____

6. Zach's taking pictures. _____

7. Kate's standing in line. _____

8. Claudia's eating lunch. _____

2. Listening

🔊 Kate is busy today. Where is she? Listen and number the sentences from 1 to 4.

She's in the park. _____   She's at the movie theater. _____

She's in a store. _____   She's in school. _____

3. Game What Are They Doing?

A Look at the picture for one minute. Then cover the picture, and read the sentences. Check (✓) T (true) or F (false).

	T	F
1. Paul is buying a baseball glove.	☐	☑
2. Sarah is watching TV.	☐	☐
3. Kevin is wearing a helmet.	☐	☐
4. Ann is doing karate.	☐	☐
5. Will is throwing trash in the trash can.	☐	☐
6. Ms. Kean and Mr. Cardoso are taking pictures.	☐	☐
7. Dmitri is talking on the phone.	☐	☐
8. Adam and Suzanne are swimming.	☐	☐
9. Adela is playing the violin.	☐	☐

B Work with a classmate. Close your book. Your classmate's book is open. How many things can you remember from the picture? Tell your classmate. Your classmate says *Yes* or *No*. Then switch roles.

> John is reading a book.

> No, he isn't. He's listening to music.

Lesson 23 At the beach

1. Vocabulary

🔊 **A** What are these people doing at the beach? Match the two parts of each sentence. Then listen and practice.

1. Two boys are _h_   a. collecting seashells.
2. A baby is ____   b. floating on a raft.
3. Two girls are ____   c. flying a kite.
4. A family is ____   d. having a picnic.
5. A dog is ____   e. playing in the sand.
6. A man is ____   f. sailing a boat.
7. A boy is ____   g. swimming in the ocean.
8. A girl is ____   h. throwing a Frisbee® disc.

B What do you do at the beach? Write sentences about two things you do and two things you don't do.

Things I do at the beach	Things I don't do at the beach
I swim in the ocean.	I don't collect seashells.
_____	_____
_____	_____

2. Language focus

🔊 **A** Mike and Ellen look for each other at the beach. Listen and practice.

Ellen Hi, Mike. It's Ellen. I'm at the beach. Where are you?

Mike Hi, Ellen. I'm at the beach, too.

Ellen Really? I'm sitting near a lifeguard chair.

Mike Hmm. Me, too. I don't see you, but I see a little girl in a red bathing suit.

Ellen Me, too. Is she playing in the sand?

Mike No, she isn't. She's collecting seashells.

Ellen Seashells? I guess there are a lot of girls in red bathing suits here today!

Present continuous
Yes / No questions

Is she **playing** in the sand?
  Yes, she **is**.
  No, she **isn't**.
Are they **throwing** a Frisbee® disc?
  Yes, they **are**.
  No, they **aren't**.

🔊 **B** Complete the rest of the conversation. Listen and check. Then practice.

Ellen OK, are you sitting near two boys?

Mike Yes, I ____*am*____ .

Ellen _____ they _____ a Frisbee® disc?

Mike No, they _____ . They're eating lunch on the beach.

Ellen Hmm. _____ a boy _____ a kite?

Mike Um, no. Do you see two girls near the ocean?

Ellen Yes, I do.

Mike _____ they _____ seashells?

Ellen _____, they aren't. They're having a picnic. Hey! _____ we talking about the same beach?

3. Listening

🔊 Lee calls Hannah from the beach. Are these sentences true or false? Listen and check (✓) T (true) or F (false).

	T	F
1. Naomi is swimming in the ocean.	✓	☐
2. Tom and Ken are playing ball.	☐	☐
3. Dave is sailing a boat.	☐	☐
4. Megan is floating on a raft.	☐	☐
5. Lee is taking a boat ride.	☐	☐
6. Hannah is doing homework now.	☐	☐

At the store

1. Vocabulary

◁)) **A** Ana, Clara, Rafael, Zach, and Tommy are at the store.
Listen and practice.

1. Ana and Clara are shopping for jewelry.

2. Rafael is trying on a jacket.

3. Zach is paying for a baseball glove.

4. Tommy is looking at comic books.

◁)) **B** Look at the items for sale at the store. Listen and practice.

1. a bracelet   2. a coat   3. a tennis racket   4. a surfboard   5. a ring

6. a scarf   7. a necklace   8. a belt   9. a baseball bat

C Where do the things in part B belong? Write the name of each
item in the correct column.

Jewelry	Clothes	Sports equipment
bracelet		

2. Language focus

A Ana sees Zach at the store.
Listen and practice.

> **Zach** Hi, Ana. What are you doing?
>
> **Ana** I'm here with Clara. We're shopping for jewelry. How about you?
>
> **Zach** Oh, I'm just looking at everything here.
>
> **Ana** Rafael and Tommy are here, too.
>
> **Zach** Really? What are they doing?
>
> **Ana** Well, Tommy's looking at comic books, and Rafael's trying on clothes.
>
> **Zach** Oh. What's he trying on?
>
> **Ana** He's trying on a jacket. It's red and black. It's really cool.
>
> **Zach** I have a red and black jacket, too. Hey, Rafael! That's my jacket!

Present continuous *What* questions
What are you **doing?**
I**'m looking at** everything.
What are you **doing?**
We**'re shopping for** jewelry.
What's he **trying on?**
He**'s trying on** a jacket.
What are they **doing?**
They**'re looking at** comic books.

B The friends continue to shop. Write questions.
Listen and check. Then practice.

1. **Tommy** _What's Ana trying on?_ (Ana / try on)
   Rafael She's trying on a bracelet.
2. **Rafael** _____ (you / look at)
   Ana We're looking at some jewelry.
3. **Ana** _____ (you / do)
   Zach I'm shopping for a surfboard.
4. **Clara** _____ (Rafael / pay for)
   Tommy He's paying for a belt.
5. **Zach** _____ (Ana and Clara / try on)
   Tommy They're trying on some clothes.

3. Pronunciation Stress

Listen. Notice the stress. Then listen again and practice.

> **What** are you **doing**?   **What's** he trying **on**?
>
> **What** are you **looking** for?   **What's** she **buying**?

4. Speaking

Work with a classmate. Name two of your family members.
Ask and answer questions about what they are doing now.

> I have a sister.   What's she doing now?   She's studying.

25 Connections

1. Reading

What is virtual reality?

Cool Corner... by Chris Carver

Welcome to Cool Corner! In this week's column, I'm writing about Virtual World at the State Fair.

Virtual World is not a video game – it's virtual reality. You put on a special helmet, look through high-tech goggles, and immediately you're in another world! At Virtual World, there's a virtual tour of Paris. Imagine this: You're standing in an empty room, but with the special helmet and goggles, you feel like you're standing in Paris! Tourists are taking a boat ride. A musician is playing the violin on the sidewalk, and artists are painting pictures. People are eating in cafés. Families are buying souvenirs. People are standing in line at the Eiffel Tower. It's great! You can almost smell the fresh French bread. And then, when you turn your head, you're looking at . . . No, wait. Visit Virtual World and see for yourself!

Virtual World is open every day this week from 3:00 P.M. to 10:00 P.M.

A Read the article about Virtual World.

B Are these sentences true or false? Check (✓) T (true) or F (false).

	T	F
1. Chris Carver is writing about Virtual World.	✓	
2. Virtual World is a video game.		
3. People are taking pictures of the Eiffel Tower.		
4. Tourists are taking a boat ride.		
5. Artists are painting pictures.		
6. People are eating in the picnic area.		
7. Virtual World is open in the morning.		

2. Listening

🔊 Evan is at Virtual World. He's telling his brother about what he sees. Listen and check (✓) the correct information.

1. Evan is looking at _____ .
   ☐ New York   ☑ London

2. Teens are wearing _____ clothes.
   ☐ cool   ☐ crazy

3. Some people are visiting _____ .
   ☐ a museum   ☐ a café

4. They're _____ paintings.
   ☐ looking at   ☐ buying

5. People are shopping. They're buying _____ .
   ☐ new clothes ☐ big bags

6. Some girls are _____ .
   ☐ laughing   ☐ waving

7. Evan is saying _____ to the girls.
   ☐ good-bye   ☐ hello

3. Writing

A Think of a city to visit in Virtual World. Write about some things that you see there.

City:
What are you looking at?
What are people doing?

B Now write an article for Cool Corner about the city in part A.

Imagine this: You're standing . . .

Review

Language chart review

Present continuous statements	
Affirmative	**Negative**
I'**m buying** a bracelet.	I'**m not looking at** souvenirs.
You'**re standing** in line.	You **aren't eating** lunch.
She'**s walking** in the park.	She **isn't sleeping**.
We'**re having** a picnic.	We **aren't sitting** at the beach.
They'**re visiting** a museum.	They **aren't taking** a boat ride.

A Complete the stories. Be sure to use the correct forms of the verbs and verb phrases.

Story 1

Hi! I'm Rachel. *I'm not going to school* (I / not / go to school)

today. _____ (I / hang out) with my friend,

Lissa, today. _____ (we / go sightseeing)

in the city. Right now, _____ (we / visit)

a museum. _____ (Lissa / buy)

souvenirs, and _____ (I / stand) in line.

I'm really thirsty, so _____ (I / have) a

soda. _____ (Lissa / eat) an ice-cream

cone while we wait to go into the museum.

Story 2

Some people _____ (see) a show, but

one man _____ (not / listen) to the

actors. He _____ (not / follow) the

theater's rules. He _____ (not / throw)

his trash in the trash can. Another man

_____ (not / watch)

the show. He's asleep!

Language chart review

B Look again at part A. Write questions and answers.

1. Rachel and Lissa / visit a museum today

   Q: *Are Rachel and Lissa visiting a museum today?*   **A:** *Yes, they are.*

2. Lissa / stand in line

   Q: _____   **A:** _____

3. Rachel / wear jeans

   Q: _____   **A:** _____

4. the people / see a show

   Q: _____   **A:** _____

5. the man / talk on the phone

   Q: _____   **A:** _____

C Write questions to complete the conversations.

1. **A** *What are your friends doing?*
   B My friends? They're throwing a Frisbee® disc in the yard.

2. **A** _____
   B No, we aren't eating. We're doing homework.

3. **A** _____
   B He's wearing jeans.

4. **A** _____
   B My mom's painting the kitchen.

5. **A** _____
   B I'm eating a sandwich. I'm hungry!

6. **A** _____
   B They're listening to rock music.

Where are you going?

Unit 6 **Entertainment**

1. Vocabulary

🔊 **A** Look at these events. Complete the sentences with the words in the box. Then listen and practice.

☑ amazing **robots**   ☐ fascinating **animals**   ☐ popular **movies**
☐ awesome **musicians**   ☐ incredible **teams**   ☐ thrilling **shows**

1. _Amazing robots_ walk and talk!

2. These _____ are fun for children and adults!

3. Learn about these _____ _____ .

4. See six _____ _____ for only $18.00.

5. Two _____ _____ play on Saturday.

6. _____ play rock and country music!

B Complete the sentences with your opinions. Then tell a classmate.

1. _Roberto Carlos_ is an incredible athlete.

2. _____ is a popular song.

3. _____ are amazing animals.

4. _____ is an awesome singer.

5. _____ is a fascinating class.

6. _____ is a thrilling movie.

> Roberto Carlos is an incredible athlete.

2. Language focus

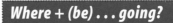

A Claudia and her little brother, Oscar, meet Rafael. They talk about where they are going. Listen and practice.

Where + (be) . . . going?

Where are you **going**?
I**'m going** to the basketball game.
We**'re going** to the Nature Center.

Rafael Claudia! Oscar!
Claudia Rafael? What a surprise!
Where are you going?
Rafael I'm going to the basketball game. I want to see the Rockets. They're an incredible team!
Claudia Yeah, I know! They're awesome!
Rafael How about you two? Where are you going?
Claudia We're going to the Nature Center.
Oscar There's a bat exhibit today!
Rafael Really? Do you like bats?
Claudia I hate bats, but Oscar thinks they're fascinating.

B Where are these people going? Write questions and answers. Listen and check. Then practice.

1. **Q:** *Where's he going?*
A: *He's going to the movies.*

2. **Q:** _____
A: _____

3. **Q:** _____
A: _____

4. **Q:** _____
A: _____

5. **Q:** _____
A: _____

6. **Q:** _____
A: _____

3. Listening

Where are these people going? Listen and check (✓) the correct information.

1. Joanne ☐ to a concert ☐ to her piano lesson
2. Jerome ☐ home ☐ to soccer practice
3. Cynthia ☐ to the library ☐ to Sarah's house
4. Ruben ☐ to the circus ☐ to the beach

Entertainment 73

Lesson 27 Birthday parties!

1. Vocabulary

◁)) **A** What do these people like to do on their birthdays?
Complete the sentences with the verb phrases in the box.
Then listen and practice.

> ☐ celebrate at a restaurant ☐ have a barbecue ☐ play cards ☐ relax at home
> ☑ eat cake ☐ open presents ☐ play party games ☐ sing songs

1. Sarah likes to
   eat cake .

2. Tim likes to ____
   _____ .

3. Diana likes to ____
   _____ .

4. Greg likes to ____
   _____ .

5. Paul likes to ____
   _____ .

6. Jack likes to ____
   _____ .

7. Rita likes to ____
   _____ .

8. Hilary likes to ____
   _____ .

B Play a chain game. Find out what your classmates like to do on
their birthdays.

Yumi What do you like to do on your birthday, Mario?
Mario I like to open presents.

└──➤ Mario What do you like to do on your birthday, Leah?
      Leah I like to play cards and sing songs with my friends.

      └──➤ Leah What do you like to do on your birthday, . . . ?

2. Language focus

◁)) **A** It's Rita's birthday. How is her family celebrating? Listen and practice.

Simple present vs. present continuous
My mom usually **cooks**. My dad **is cooking** hot dogs now.

We usually eat in the kitchen, but not today. My mom usually cooks. But my dad is cooking hot dogs now. He always cooks on my birthday.

We usually eat at 6:00. But it's 7:30 now, and we're still waiting for our dinner. My dad is a good cook. But he's very slow!

◁)) **B** Rita's family is relaxing after the barbecue. What are they doing now? What do they usually do after dinner? Write sentences. Then listen and check.

NOW

8:00 P.M.

USUALLY

8:00 P.M.

1. Rita _is playing cards_ . _She usually practices the violin._

2. Mr. Cookson _____ . _____

3. Mrs. Cookson _____ . _____

4. Peter _____ . _____

5. Lucy _____ . _____

3. Listening

◁)) Tommy's aunt calls on his birthday. Does Tommy talk about what people in his family usually do or about what they are doing now? Listen and check (✓) the correct column.

	usually	now
1. Tommy's brother	☐	☐
2. Tommy's little sister	☐	☐
3. Tommy's mother	☐	☐
4. Tommy's father	☐	☐

Mini-review

1. Language check

A The sports announcers are at an ice-skating event. Complete their sentences with the correct forms of the verbs.

1. Look! Here's Mark. _He's skating_ (he / skate) across the rink.

2. _____ always _____ (he / skate) so beautifully.

3. And now _____ (he / dance) on the ice.

4. Oh! Look! _____ (he / jump)! Amazing!

5. Of course, _____ (he / practice) every day.

6. OK. Now _____ (he / wait) for his scores.

B The competition is finished. What are these people doing now? What do they usually do at night?

1. The announcers: _They're eating dinner at a restaurant._ _They usually stay home._
   (eat dinner at a restaurant)   (stay home)

2. Mark: _____ _____
   (talk to fans)   (watch TV)

3. Diana, the coach: _____ _____
   (sleep)   (read sports magazines)

2. Game X and O

A **Play the game with a classmate. Take turns.**

One person is X, and one person is O.
Classmate 1 Point to a picture.
Classmate 2 Ask *Where's / Where are* _____ *going?*
Classmate 1 Answer the question.
▷ No mistakes? Mark the picture.
▶ Mistakes? Do not mark the picture.

Continue playing until all pictures have been marked.
The player with the most pictures marked is the winner.

1  he

2 she

3 they

4  she

5  he

6 you

7 he

8  they

9  you

10 he

11 she

12  you

B **These people are all on a bus. Where are they going?**
Complete the sentences.

1. Bill *is going to the circus* _____ .

2. Jed and Mindy _____ .

3. Henry _____ .

4. Carl _____ .

5. Pierre and Paulette _____ .

Lesson 28 Let's see a movie.

1. Vocabulary

A Label the movies with the words in the box.
Then listen and practice.

> ☑ an action movie ☐ a comedy ☐ a drama
> ☐ an animated movie ☐ a documentary ☐ a horror movie

1. This is *an action movie* .

2. This is _____ .

3. This is _____ .

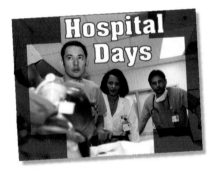

4. This is _____ .

5. This is _____ .

6. This is _____ .

B Write the plural form of each kind of movie. Then write your opinion using *like* or *don't like*.

Singular	Plural	Your opinion
1. a comedy	*comedies*	*I like comedies.*
2. a horror movie		
3. an action movie		
4. a drama		
5. a documentary		
6. an animated movie		

2. Language focus

📢 **A** Rafael invites Ana to a movie.
Listen and practice.

Rafael I want to go to the movies tonight.
Do you want to come?

Ana Well, what do you want to see?

Rafael I want to see a horror movie –
Late at Night. It's a new movie.
It's very popular. Julia James
is in it. She's awesome!

Ana Well, thanks, but I don't want to see a horror
movie. I want to stay home and watch TV.

📢 **B** Now Rafael invites Kate. Complete the conversation.
Listen and check. Then practice.

Rafael _Do_ you _want to_ go to the movies?

Kate No. I _____ to the movies.

Rafael Are you sure? I want to see *Late at Night.*

Kate Sorry. I really _____ go.

Rafael OK. _____ you _____
a drama on TV?

Kate No. I don't like dramas.

Rafael Well, what _____ you _____ do?

Kate I _____ stay home and sleep.

3. Pronunciation Reduction

📢 **LIsten. Notice how *want to* is reduced in conversation. Then listen
again and practice.**

I **wanna** see an action movie.

They **wanna** go to the concert.

We **wanna** have a picnic.

I **wanna** play video games.

4. Listening

📢 What does each person want to see? Listen and check (✓) the
correct kind of movie.

	a comedy	a horror movie	an action movie	a drama	a documentary	an animated movie
1. Ted	☐	☐	☐	☐	☐	☐
2. Joe	☐	☐	☐	☐	☐	☐
3. Maggie	☐	☐	☐	☐	☐	☐
4. Connie	☐	☐	☐	☐	☐	☐

(29) In line at the movies

1. Vocabulary

🔊 **A** Read the descriptions and look at the people waiting in line at the movies. Write the correct name next to each person. Then listen and practice.

- ☐ Carlos is tall and slim. He has wavy, black hair.
- ☐ Carolyn is short and heavy. She has short, straight, red hair.
- ☐ David is short and slim. He has curly, black hair and blue eyes.
- ☐ Kevin is average height. He has short, brown hair.
- ☐ Marci is average height. She has medium-length hair and brown eyes.
- ☑ Sandra is tall and slim. She has long, blond hair.

B Complete the chart. Use the words from part A.

Height	Body type	Hair length	Hairstyle	Hair color	Eye color
tall	slim	long	curly	blond	blue

2. Language focus

🔊 **A** Marci and Sandra are still in line at the movies. They're waiting for Sandra's friend, John. Listen and practice.

Sandra Where's John? I don't see him. The show starts at 2:20!

Marci What does John look like?

Sandra He's tall and slim.

Marci What color is his hair?

Sandra It's blond. He has short, curly hair.

Marci I think I see him. He's near the end of the line. He's talking to a girl.

Sandra What does the girl look like?

Marci She has long, brown hair, and she's wearing a yellow blouse. Do you see her? She's cute.

Sandra Yes, I see her. I see John, too! He's not looking for *us*. I guess he's too busy!

What questions about people
What does John look like?
He's tall and slim.
He has short, curly hair.
He has brown eyes.
What's his hair like?
It's short and curly.
What color is his hair?
It's blond.
What color are his eyes?
They're blue.

Admission

🔊 **B** Look at the picture of Carolyn in 1A. Write a question for each answer. Then listen and check.

1. _What does she look like?_   She's short and heavy.

2. _____ It's short and straight.

3. _____ It's red.

4. _____ They're brown.

C Complete the questions with names of your classmates. Then write answers.

1. (boy) What does _____ look like? _____

2. (boy) What color is _____'s hair? _____

3. (girl) What's _____'s hair like? _____

4. (girl) What color are _____'s eyes? _____

3. Speaking

Play a game. Think of a teacher in your school. Your classmates ask questions and guess.

Classmate 1 Is it a man or a woman?
You It's a man.

Classmate 2 What color is his hair?
You It's blond.

Classmate 3 Is it curly?
You No. It's short and straight.

Classmate 4 Is it Mr. Santos?
You Yes, it is!

30 Connections

1. Reading

Do you know what a hypnotist is?

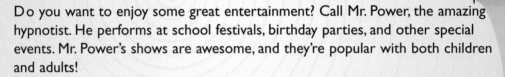

MR. POWER
THE AMAZING HYPNOTIST

Do you want to enjoy some great entertainment? Call Mr. Power, the amazing hypnotist. He performs at school festivals, birthday parties, and other special events. Mr. Power's shows are awesome, and they're popular with both children and adults!

There's always a lot of action at Mr. Power's shows. People walk like dogs. They dance weird dances. They sing songs in different languages. These shows are crazy! But don't worry – they're safe! You can't do anything scary or dangerous.

Read what these people say about Mr. Power's shows:

"I'm a big fan! I go to his shows every month. They're very enjoyable." – Ms. Miller
"His shows are awesome! I laugh until I cry — every time I go." – Bobby Carson

CALL MR. POWER TODAY!

A Read the article about Mr. Power.

B Are these sentences true or false? Check (✓) T (true) or F (false). Then correct the false sentences.

	T	F
1. Mr. Power doesn't perform at birthday parties. *Mr. Power performs at birthday parties.*	☐	☑
2. Mr. Power's shows aren't popular with adults.	☐	☐
3. Mr. Power's shows aren't dangerous.	☐	☐
4. Ms. Miller hardly ever goes to his shows.	☐	☐
5. Bobby Carson doesn't like the shows.	☐	☐

2. Listening

🔊 **Bobby Carson is in Mr. Power's show. Listen and check (✓) the correct sentences.**

1. ☑ Bobby is tall.
   ☐ Bobby is short.

2. ☐ Bobby is playing the guitar now.
   ☐ Bobby plays the guitar.

3. ☐ Bobby usually goes to bed at 11:30 P.M.
   ☐ Bobby is sleeping.

4. ☐ Bobby is shooting the ball.
   ☐ Bobby is catching the ball.

5. ☐ Bobby is good at dancing.
   ☐ Bobby isn't good at dancing.

6. ☐ Mr. Power wants to stop.
   ☐ Mr. Power doesn't want to stop.

3. Writing

A Imagine you are a hypnotist. Think of things for a person to do. Write them on the list.

1. dance	4.
2.	5.
3.	6.

B Now write a script to read to a volunteer at the show. Use the example to help you.

Lisa, you are tired, very tired. Now you are a dancer.

You like to dance. You're dancing right now.

Review

Language chart review

Where + (be) . . . going?	*want / don't want + to (verb)*

Where are you **going**?
  I**'m going** to the circus.
  We**'re going** home.
 	
Where's Sarah **going**?
  She**'s going** to the concert.
	Do you **want to come** to my house?
	  Yes, I **do**. / No, I **don't**.
	
	What **do** you **want to do**?
	  I **want to stay** home tonight.
	  I **don't want to go** out.

A Jason Daniels from *Connect! TV News* talks to teens for a report called "Where Are You Going?" Complete the conversation with the correct forms of the verbs.

Jason Hey, kids! *Where are you going?*

    (where / you / go?)

Brian _____

    (I / go / to my karate class.)

Jason _____

    (where / your friend / go?)

Brian _____

    (she / go / to the mall.)

Zoe Yeah, I want to find some new sneakers.

Jason Awesome!

Jason And _____

    (where / you / go?)

Terry _____

    (we / go / to the movies.)

Jason _____

    (what / you / want / to see?)

Terry We want to see the new James Bond movie.

    Hey, Jason! _____

    (you / want / to come / with us?)

Jason No, thanks. But have fun!

Language chart review

Simple present vs. present continuous	*What* questions about people	
I usually **practice** the piano after school.	**What does Claire look like?** She's short and slim. She has long, brown hair.	**What color is her hair?** It's black.
Today, I**'m reading** a book.		
We usually **sing** songs in music class.	**What's her hair like?** It's long and straight.	**What color are her eyes?** They're brown.
Today, we**'re listening** to CDs.		

B Complete the sentences. Use the correct forms of the words in the box.

> eat   play   talk   wear

1. My name's Eddie. I usually _____wear_____ jeans, but today I'm _____wearing_____ nice clothes. I always _____ nice clothes on my birthday.

2. Ramon is usually very shy. He hardly ever _____ in class, but today he's _____ a lot.

3. I'm Grace, and this is my family. We usually _____ dinner at home, but today is special. We're _____ in a restaurant. The cake at this restaurant is great!

4. Paula is _____ cards with Tony right now. They usually _____ cards on Sunday, but this week they're _____ on Saturday.

C Complete the conversations.

1. **Joe** My cousin wants to visit me. She wants to come in December.
   Lee Cool! What ___does___ she ___look___ like?
   Joe _____ pretty. _____ tall and slim. She _____ short, red _____ .
   Lee _____ color _____ her eyes?
   Joe _____ blue.

2. **Cara** There's a new boy in my class.
   Dora Really? What _____ he look _____ ?
   Cara _____ cute. He's short _____ heavy.
   Dora _____ his hair like?
   Cara He _____ curly, brown hair. Oh, and _____ eyes _____ brown.

3. **Val** I think my brother is in your English class.
   Dina Really? What _____ he _____ like?
   Val _____ tall and slim.
   Dina A lot of boys in the class are tall and slim!
   Val He _____ black hair, and _____ eyes _____ black, too.
   Dina Oh, I know him!

Lesson 31 I'm hungry!

1. Vocabulary

🔊 **A** Look at the food in the kitchen. Label the pictures with the words in the box. Then listen and practice.

☐ apples	☐ broccoli	☐ cheese	☐ meat	☑ rice
☐ bananas	☐ butter	☐ eggs	☐ potatoes	☐ water

1. _rice_
2.
3.
4.
5.
6.
7.
8.
9.
10.

B How often do you eat or drink the items in part A at lunchtime? Write the items in the correct columns. Then tell your classmates.

always	sometimes	never
	rice	

> I sometimes eat rice.

2. Language focus

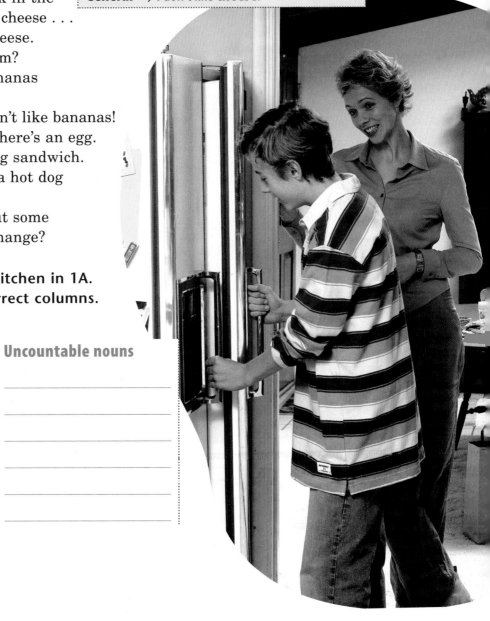

Countable and uncountable nouns
Countable nouns (things you can count)
Specific → There's **an egg** in the refrigerator.
General → I like **eggs**.
Uncountable nouns (things you cannot count)
Specific → There's **cheese** in the refrigerator.
General → I don't like **cheese**.

A Zach is hungry.
Listen and practice.

Zach Hey, Mom! I'm hungry,
but there's nothing to eat.

Mom Nothing to eat? Look in the
refrigerator. There's cheese . . .

Zach Yuck! I don't like cheese.
Do we have ice cream?

Mom No, but we have bananas
and apples, and . . .

Zach Mom, you know I don't like bananas!

Mom What about eggs? There's an egg.
You can make an egg sandwich.

Zach No, thanks. I want a hot dog
or a cookie.

Mom Oh, Zach. How about some
healthy food for a change?

B Look at the items in the kitchen in 1A.
Write the items in the correct columns.
Then listen and check.

Countable nouns	Uncountable nouns
eggs	

3. Speaking

Play a chain game. Learn about the foods your classmates like and
the foods they don't like.

Mario I like cheese. I don't like broccoli. How about you, Yumi?

    → **Yumi** I like pizza. I don't like meat. How about you, Camilo?

        → **Camilo** I like apples. I don't like bananas. How about you, Leah?

           → **Leah** I like rice. I don't like apples. How about you, . . . ?

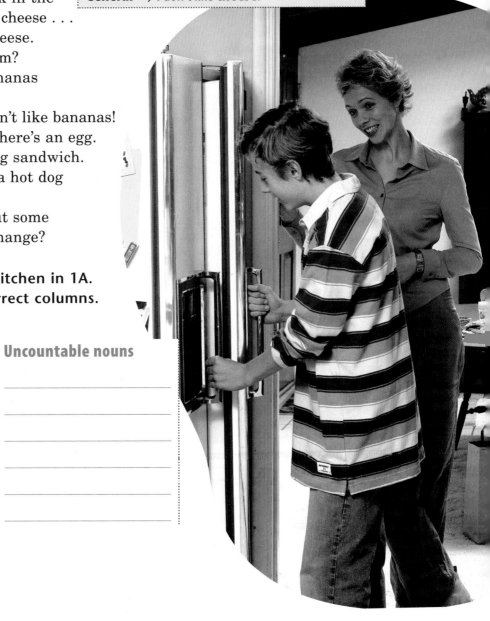

Lesson 32 Picnic plans

1. Vocabulary

🔊 **A** Ana and Rafael plan a picnic. Listen and practice.

1. milk
3. juice
2. cups
4. bread
6. fruit
5. plates
7. pasta
8. spoons
9. forks
10. knives

B Where do the items in part A belong? Write the items in the correct columns.

Food	Drinks	Supplies
		cups

2. Language focus

A The friends decide what they need for their picnic. Listen and practice.

Rafael OK, what do we need for the picnic? Um, how many cups do we have?

Ana Let's see. We have about 20 cups. But there are only 3 plates. We need plates.

Rafael OK. What about food? How much pasta is there?

Ana Um, there's a little pasta. We need pasta and a lot of milk. There's a little bread, but let's buy bread, too.

Rafael What else? How much juice do we have?

Ana I think we have a lot of juice.

Rafael Wait! Look at Zach! We need juice *now*!

How much / How many . . . ?
Countable nouns
How many cups do we have?
We have **20** cup**s**.
We have **a lot of** cup**s**.
There are **3** plate**s**.
There are **a few** plate**s**.
Uncountable nouns
How much pasta is there?
There's **a lot of** pasta.
There's **a little** pasta.

B Look at the photos. Complete the questions and answers. Listen and check. Then practice.

1. **Q:** *How many spoons are there?*
   A: There are 4 spoons.

2. **Q:** _____
   A: There's a little juice.

3. **Q:** _____
   A: There are 3 cups.

4. **Q:** How much fruit is there?
   A: _____

5. **Q:** How many knives are there?
   A: _____

6. **Q:** How much bread is there?
   A: _____

3. Listening

Another group plans a picnic. How much or how many of each thing do they need? Write the number or check (✓) the correct column.

	Number	a few	a little	a lot
1. hot dogs	25	☐	☐	☐
2. fruit	___	☐	☐	☐
3. cheese	___	☐	☐	☐
4. pasta	___	☐	☐	☐
5. cups	___	☐	☐	☐
6. cookies	___	☐	☐	☐

What We Eat 89

Mini-review

1. Language check

A Which of these items do you eat or drink? Which don't you eat or drink? Write sentences in the correct columns.

☐ pasta   ☐ bananas
☑ eggs   ☐ ice cream   ☐ butter
☐ hamburgers   ☐ milk   ☐ juice
☐ broccoli   ☐ bread   ☐ potatoes
☐ hot dogs   ☑ meat   ☐ apples
☐ rice   ☐ water

Eat		Drink	
I eat eggs.			
I don't eat meat.			

B Answer these questions about yourself. Write a number or use *a lot*, *a little*, or *a few*.

1. How much rice do you eat in a week?

   I eat a lot of rice.

2. How many books do you have in your bag?

   _____

3. How much homework do you do every day?

   _____

4. How many T-shirts do you have?

   _____

5. How many magazines do you read in a month?

   _____

6. How much TV do you watch in a week?

   _____

2. Game Food Puzzle

Work with a partner. Look at the photos. Guess the names of the items, and label the photos. Then write the names of the food items to complete the puzzle. The pair that finishes first is the winner.

ACROSS

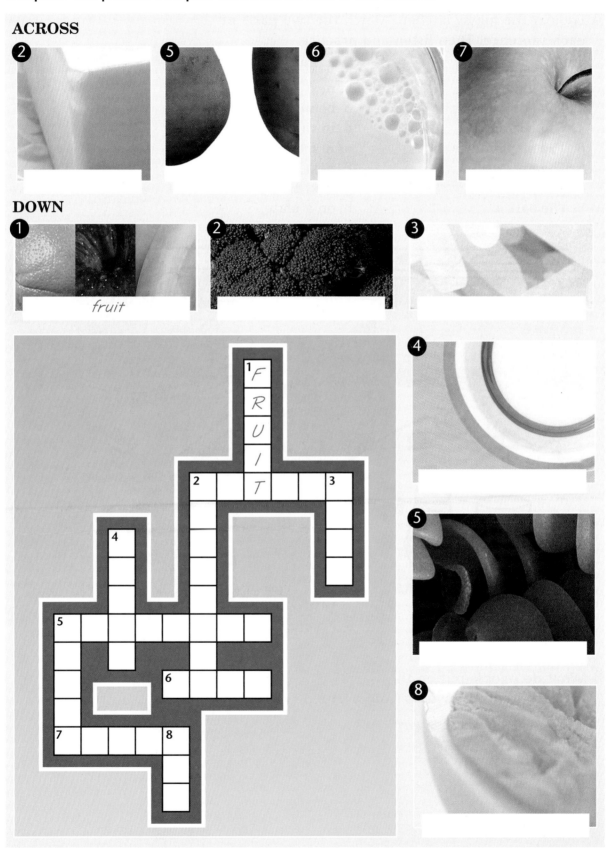

DOWN

fruit

Lesson 33 A snack

1. Vocabulary

🔊 **A** Look at the messy kitchen. Match the two parts of each sentence. Then listen and practice.

1. The ham is ___e___   a. next to the salt.
2. The jelly is _____   b. next to the jelly.
3. The ketchup is _____   c. behind the ham.
4. The lettuce is _____   d. in the cabinet.
5. The mayonnaise is _____   e. in front of the ketchup.
6. The mustard is _____   f. next to the pepper.
7. The pepper is _____   g. next to the mustard.
8. The salt is _____   h. on a plate.

B What do people put on the food items below? Write two things for each item. Use words from part A or your own ideas.

1. sandwich: _mustard, lettuce_____

2. eggs: _____

3. hamburger: _____

4. hot dog: _____

5. meat: _____

2. Language focus

A Laura makes a sandwich. Listen and practice.

Laura I'm hungry. Let's make a sandwich!

Ted Good idea. I'm hungry, too.

Laura Um, there's some ham here.

Ted Good! I like ham sandwiches.

Laura There's some mustard, but there isn't any mayonnaise.

Ted That's OK. Mustard is fine.

Laura There's some pepper. Oh, no! There aren't any potatoes!

Ted What? Potatoes on a sandwich?

Laura Sure! Oh, look! There are some bananas . . .

Ted What kind of sandwich is that?

Laura It's my favorite! Do you want one?

Ted No, thanks. I'm not hungry now.

some / any
Countable nouns
There **are some** bananas.
There **aren't any** potatoes.
Uncountable nouns
There**'s some** mustard.
There **isn't any** mayonnaise.

B Look at the photos. Write sentences with *some* or *any*. Then listen and check.

1. *There isn't any salt.*
   (salt)

2.  _____
   (mustard)

3.  _____
   (eggs)

4. _____
   (ham)

5. _____
   (apples)

6.  _____
   (cups)

7.  _____
   (bananas)

8.  _____
   (ketchup)

3. Speaking

Think of your refrigerator. Tell a classmate what is and what isn't in it. Use the words in the box or your own ideas.

> There's some juice. There isn't any water.

> There's some ice cream. There isn't any mustard.

juice   milk   ice cream
eggs   ketchup   mustard
meat   apples   ham   water

Lesson 34 On the menu

1. Vocabulary

A Look at the restaurant menu. Write the names of the items in the correct places on the menu. Then listen and practice.

Bob's DINER
Lunch Menu

Appetizers
salad $3.00
black bean soup $2.50
_____ $2.50

Main Dishes
hamburger $4.50
_____ $5.00
_____ $5.00
chicken sandwich $6.00
today's fish $4.50
rice and beans with meat. $6.50

☐ baked potato ☐ black bean soup ☐ cheeseburger

☐ steak sandwich ☐ vegetable soup

Side Orders
french fries $2.00
_____ $1.50

Desserts
ice cream $1.50
cookies $1.00
_____ $2.00
_____ $2.00
_____ $2.00

Drinks
soda $1.50
_____ $2.00
milk $1.00
_____ $2.00

☐ carrot cake ☐ chocolate cake ☐ iced tea

☐ milk shake ☐ pie

B What are some of your favorite foods in a restaurant?
Complete the chart. Then compare with your classmates.

Favorite appetizer	_____
Favorite main dish	_____
Favorite side order	_____
Favorite dessert	_____
Favorite drink	_____

What's your favorite appetizer?

My favorite appetizer is . . .

2. Language focus

🔊 **A** Tommy orders lunch. Listen and practice.

would like

I**'d like** vegetable soup, please.
Would you **like** a drink?
    Yes, please. I**'d like** some water.
    No, thanks.

I'd = I would

Waitress	Hi. Are you ready to order?
Tommy	Yes, I am.
Waitress	OK. Would you like an appetizer?
Tommy	Yes. I'd like vegetable soup, please.
Waitress	OK. What else?
Tommy	I'd like a chicken sandwich, please.
Waitress	And would you like a side order?
Tommy	No, thanks.
Waitress	Would you like a drink?
Tommy	Yes, please. I'd like a milk shake and some water. I'm really thirsty!

🔊 **B** Tommy orders dessert. Complete the conversation. Listen and check. Then practice.

Waitress	*Would you like* anything else?
Tommy	Yes. _____ some cake.
Waitress	What kind of cake _____ you _____ ?
Tommy	_____ chocolate cake. And _____ some ice cream, too, please.
Waitress	OK.
Tommy	Oh! _____ some cookies, too.
Waitress	Wow! That's a lot of dessert!

3. Pronunciation Intonation

🔊 Listen. Notice the intonation. Listen again and practice.

Would you like a hamburger?   Would you like some milk?

Would you like some french fries?   Would you like some ice cream?

4. Listening

🔊 What do Ana, Kate, Rafael, and Zach order? Listen and write *A* (Ana), *K* (Kate), *R* (Rafael), or *Z* (Zach).

What We Eat 95

35 Connections

1. Reading

How many hot dogs can you eat?

FOOD CONTESTS

A lot of people eat one hot dog at a meal. But Takeru Kobayashi of Japan can eat 44 – in just 12 minutes! That's a lot of hot dogs! Kobayashi was the winner of the 2003 world hot dog-eating contest in New York City.

The United States has really crazy eating contests. Think about these winners: Bill Simmons can eat 137 chicken wings in 30 minutes. Eric Booker can eat 15 burritos in 8 minutes and 38 eggs in 10 minutes.

How can these people eat so much food? They practice! Kobayashi practices by eating cabbage and drinking water. He says it makes his stomach bigger. But Kobayashi is not heavy – he's actually very slim.

Why do people try these contests? Booker says that eating is a sport like soccer or baseball. There are games, rules, and winners. Not everyone agrees. Some people think that eating too much just makes you sick!

◁)) **A** Read the article about food contests.

B Complete the questions with *How much* or *How many*.
Then match the questions to the correct answers.

1. *How many* hot dogs can Takeru Kobayashi eat? *d*   a. 12 minutes
2. _____ chicken wings can Bill Simmons eat? ____   b. 15 in 8 minutes
3. _____ burritos can Eric Booker eat? ____   c. 38 in 10 minutes
4. _____ eggs can Eric Booker eat? ____   d. 44
5. _____ time does it take Takeru Kobayashi   e. 137 in 30 minutes
   to eat 44 hot dogs? ____

2. Listening

🔊 **Listen to the radio announcement for the fair. Check (✓) the sentences you hear.**

1. ☑ Come to the fair this weekend! ☐ Come to the fair tomorrow!
2. ☐ There are some exciting contests this year, too. ☐ You can win some exciting contests this year, too.
3. ☐ How many can you eat? ☐ How much can you eat?
4. ☐ There's a chocolate-eating contest. ☐ There's a chocolate cake-eating contest.
5. ☐ You need a fork, a spoon, and a knife. ☐ You don't need a fork, a spoon, or a knife.
6. ☐ I can eat a lot of cake. ☐ I can't eat a lot of cake.
7. ☐ The winner gets a computer! ☐ The winner gets a chocolate cake!

3. Writing

A Look at these contests. Which contest do you want to try? Complete the chart for the contest.

Dancing Contest
Are you a good dancer? Can you dance all day? Try the dance contest! Dance for a long time, and you can win!
Saturday, April 15
3:00 P.M. — 12:00 A.M.

Art Contest
For students in grades 5 to 9. Draw a picture by April 30, and enter it in our contest. Ask your art teacher for more information. Winners get free books.

Singing Contest
Any kind of song is OK – a happy song, a sad song, a funny song, or a love song. Sing with a friend. Sing a lot of songs, or sing a few. Maybe you can win a CD or a T-shirt!

CAKE-EATING CONTEST
Do you like cake? Can you eat a lot of cake in a few minutes? Enter the cake-eating contest. Eat a lot of your favorite cake, and maybe you can win!
Friday, April 14
4:00 P.M.

Cake-Eating Contest	_____ Contest
I can _eat a lot of cake_ .	I can _____ .
I like _cake_ .	I like _____ .
Chocolate cake is my favorite _cake_ .	_____ is my favorite _____ .
I eat cake every day.	_____ every day.

B Now write about the contest and why you want to try it. Use the information in part A to help you.

I want to try the cake-eating contest. I like cake. I eat cake every day. Chocolate cake is my favorite cake. I can eat fast, too.

Review

Language chart review

Countable and uncountable nouns		
Countable		**Uncountable**
Specific There are **two apples**.		There's **broccoli** on the table.
General I love apple**s**.		I don't like **broccoli**.

How much / How many . . . ?	
With countable	**With uncountable**
How many apples do we need?	**How much** bread do we have?
We need **a few** apple**s**.	We have **a little** bread.
We need **3** apple**s**.	We have **a lot of** bread.

some / any		
Countable and uncountable		
There **are some** cups.		
There **aren't any** plates.		
There**'s some** salt.		
There **isn't any** rice.		

A Becky and Jeremy make breakfast for their family.
Complete the conversation.

Becky   Let's make breakfast.

Jeremy   Good idea. How about eggs? We all like
_____eggs_____ (eggs / ten eggs).

Becky   OK. _____ (How much / How many)
eggs do we need?

Jeremy   Well, I think we need eight eggs. And
we need _____ (a little / a few) cheese, too.

Becky   We don't have _____ (some / any) cheese.

Jeremy   Oh. So let's put _____ (a little / a few)
potatoes in the eggs.

Becky   But Mom doesn't like _____ (potatoes / the potatoes)
in her eggs.

Jeremy   That's true. How about _____ (a little / a lot)
ham? There's _____ (some / any) ham in
the refrigerator.

Becky   Yes! And let's put _____ (some / any) milk
in the eggs, too. _____ (How much / How many)
milk do we need?

Jeremy   We just need _____ (a little / a few) milk.
Do we want bread, too?

Becky   Yes, we do. And there's _____ (a lot / a lot of)
bread here.

Jeremy   OK! Let's cook!

B Write questions about Becky and Jeremy with *How much* or *How many.* Then look again at the picture in part A, and answer the questions. Use *a few, a little,* or *a lot of.*

1. milk

   Q: *How much milk do they have?*
   A: *They have a little milk.*

2. potatoes

   Q: _____
   A: _____

3. ham

   Q: _____
   A: _____

4. apples

   Q: _____
   A: _____

5. juice

   Q: _____
   A: _____

6. eggs

   Q: _____
   A: _____

Language chart review

would like
I'**d like** a sandwich.
Would you **like** a side order?
Yes, please. I'**d like** french fries.
No, thanks.

C Sandy orders lunch. Complete the questions. Then write answers. Use the sentences in the box.

☐ I'd like a ham and cheese sandwich.	☑ Yes. I'd like a sandwich.
☐ I'd like chocolate ice cream.	☐ Yes. I'd like some ice cream.
☐ No, thanks.	☐ Yes, please. I'd like apple juice.

Waiter Hi. Are you ready to order?
Sandy *Yes. I'd like a sandwich.*
Waiter What kind of sandwich *would*
  you *like* ?
Sandy _____
Waiter _____ a side dish?
  Maybe some french fries?
Sandy _____
Waiter Would you like a drink?
Sandy _____
Waiter _____ you _____ dessert?
Sandy _____
Waiter What kind of ice cream _____ ?
Sandy _____

World weather

1. Vocabulary

A Match the symbols to the sentences describing weather and temperature. Then listen and practice.

Weather

1. ☀   It's cloudy.
2. 🍃   It's rainy.
3. ❄   It's snowy.
4. ☁   It's sunny.
5. 🌧   It's windy.

Temperature

6. 🌡   It's cold.
7. 🌡   It's cool.
8. 🌡   It's hot.
9. 🌡   It's warm.

B It's December. Look at the weather map, and complete the sentences with words from part A. Then listen and practice.

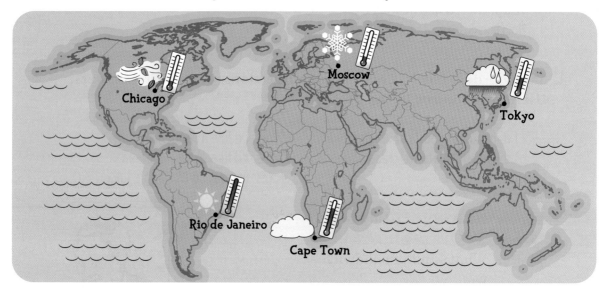

1. It's ___cold___ and ___snowy___ in Moscow.
2. It's _____ and _____ in Chicago.
3. It's _____ and _____ in Tokyo.
4. It's _____ and _____ in Rio de Janeiro.
5. It's _____ and _____ in Cape Town.

C What kind of weather do you like?
What kind of weather don't you like?
Tell your classmates.

> I like hot, sunny weather. I don't like . . .

2. Language focus

A It's Sunday afternoon. Tommy is in an online chat room. Listen and practice.

What's the weather like?

What's the weather like in April?
It's usually **rainy**.
What's the weather like today?
It's **warm** and **sunny** today.

International Chat

Tommy: Hi, everyone! I'm doing my science homework. I need information about April weather around the world.

Josie: Hi, Tommy! I can help you.

Tommy: Great! Where do you live, Josie?

Josie: In Santiago, Chile.

Tommy: What's the weather like in Santiago in April?

Josie: It's usually warm. But it's not warm today.

Tommy: What's the weather like today?

Josie: It's hot and sunny. I want to go to the park later.

Tommy: That sounds fun! Thanks for your help! Sofia, can you help me, too? Where do you live?

Now in chat room:

Tommy
Sofia
Lynn
Garth
Josie

B Complete more of Tommy's questions and answers from the chat. Listen and check. Then practice.

1. **Tommy** What's the weather like in Chicago in April?

   Sofia *It's usually warm and rainy.*

2. **Tommy** What's the weather like in New York in April?

   Lynn _____ and _____

3. **Tommy** What's the weather _____ in New York today?

   Lynn _____ and _____ today.

4. **Tommy** _____ in Winnipeg in April?

   Garth _____ and _____ .

5. **Garth** Hey, _____ in Darwin in April, Tommy?

   Tommy _____ and _____ , but it's cool and cloudy now.

3. Speaking

Work with a classmate. Ask and answer questions about the weather in your town or city in different months.

What's the weather like in Rio in February?   It's usually hot and sunny.

Lesson 37 Natural wonders

1. Vocabulary

A Complete the sentences with the words in the box.
Then listen and practice.

> ☐ the Andes Mountains ☐ the Galápagos Islands ☑ Mammoth Hot Springs
> ☐ El Yunque Rain Forest ☐ the Jenolan Caves ☐ the Mississippi River

1. _Mammoth Hot Springs_ are in Yellowstone National Park in the United States.

2. Some people live on houseboats on _____ .

3. _____ are in the Pacific Ocean.

4. _____ are in Australia.

5. _____ is in Puerto Rico.

6. People ski in _____ .

B Kate loves the outdoors. Complete her sentences with the words in the box.

> ☐ cave ☐ hot spring ☐ island ☐ mountain ☐ rain forest ☑ river

1. I want to go canoeing on a _____ river _____ .

2. I want to climb a really big _____ .

3. I want to take a boat ride around an _____ in the sea.

4. I want to take pictures of birds and other animals in a _____ .

5. I want to see the inside of a big, underground _____ .

6. I want to sit and relax in a _____ .

2. Language focus

can (for possibility)

You can see a lot of amazing things.
What **can you** see on this trail?
  You can see some incredible mountains.
Can you buy any food around here?
Yes, **you can**.
No, **you can't**.

Guide You can see a lot of amazing things in this park.

Kate So, what can you see on this trail?

Guide You can see some incredible mountains, hot springs, rivers . . .

Kate Can you see any animals?

Guide Yes, you can. You can see snakes and wolves. And sometimes you can see bears.

Kate I don't want to see any bears right now!

Guide And they don't want to see you!

Kate I'm hungry. Can you buy any food around here?

Guide No, you can't. You can buy food at hotels and at the souvenir shops. You were supposed to bring lunch!

Kate Oh, no! I forgot!

◁)) **B** What can you do at these parks? Look at the chart, and write sentences. Then listen and check.

Park Facilities and Activities	🛶	🐎	⛺	🐦	🏊
Kent Park	✓		✓	✓	
Ranch Park		✓	✓		
Thunder Park	✓			✓	✓

1. (Kent Park) *You can go canoeing. You can go camping. You can see birds.*

2. (Ranch Park) _____

3. (Thunder Park) _____

3. Listening

◁)) Can people do these activities near Kate's hometown? Listen and check (✓) Yes or No.

	Yes	No
1. go canoeing	✓	☐
2. climb mountains	☐	☐
3. visit caves	☐	☐
4. go to hot springs	☐	☐
5. go dancing	☐	☐

Mini-review

1. Language check

Seth and his father talk about vacation plans. Complete their conversation with *you can*, *you can't*, *what can you*, and *can you*.

Seth I don't know, Dad. The park sounds a little boring.

Mr. Tellis Boring? The park sounds really interesting!

Seth But _what can you_ do there?

Mr. Tellis _____ do a lot of things. _____ hike and camp . . .

Seth You can hike and camp here in our town!

Mr. Tellis Yes, _____ . But _____ climb mountains in our town? _____ see caves in our town?

Seth No, _____ . Maybe the park is OK. _____ see bats in the caves?

Mr. Tellis Yes, and _____ see them fly out of the caves at night. There's also a great beach.

Seth _____ do at the beach?

Mr. Tellis _____ go swimming. Or _____ take a boat ride to an island.

Seth OK. I want to go. Let's tell Mom we have a plan!

2. Listening

🔊 Seth and his father watch *Adventure Vacations* on TV. This week's show is in northern Japan. Listen and number these places as the guide talks about them.

_____ cave

_____ hot spring

_____ island

_1_ mountain

_____ river

3. Game Weather

Play the game with a classmate. Use things in your bag as game markers. Take turns.

Classmate 1 Close your eyes and touch one of the numbers. Move your marker that number of spaces.

Classmate 2 Ask a question about the weather, using the word in the space.

Classmate 1 Answer the question.

June. What's the weather like in June? It's usually warm and rainy.

Lesson 38 World of friends

1. Vocabulary

🔊 **A** Can you say "hello" in other languages? Match the languages to the correct greetings. Then listen and practice.

1. Arabic _c_   a. Guten Tag!   4. Italian _____   d. Olá!

2. German _____   b. Geia sou!   5. Portuguese _____ e. Zdravstvuite!

3. Greek _____   c. Ahalan!   6. Russian _____   f. Buon giorno!

🔊 **B** Tommy meets a lot of friends online. Where are they from? Complete their sentences with the words in the box. Then listen and practice.

☐ Germany   ☐ Greece   ☐ Italy   ☑ Morocco   ☐ Portugal   ☐ Russia

1. My name is Khalil. I live in _Morocco_ . "Ahalan!"

2. I'm Karl. I live in _____ . "Guten Tag!"

3. "Buon giorno!" I'm Carlotta. I live in _____ .

4. "Geia sou!" I'm Christina. I live in _____ .

5. I'm Ivan. I live in _____ . "Zdravstvuite!"

6. I'm Emilia. I live in _____ . "Olá!"

C Work with a classmate. Look at part B. Ask and answer questions about where Tommy's friends are from and what languages they speak.

Is Ivan from Russia?

Does Emilia speak Italian?

Yes, he is.

No, she doesn't. She speaks Portuguese.

2. Language focus

Who + (verb)...?
Who lives in Italy?
Carlotta **does.**
Who plays soccer?
Karl and Emilia **do.**

A Claudia wants new e-pals. She asks Tommy about his online friends. Listen and practice.

Claudia Can you help me find some new e-pals?

Tommy Well, maybe you can write to my e-pals. Karl, Emilia, Ivan, and Carlotta are really interesting.

Claudia Do they like sports?

Tommy Sure. One of them plays tennis, two of them play soccer, and . . .

Claudia Who plays soccer?

Tommy Karl and Emilia do. Karl lives in Germany. The others live in Greece, Morocco, Italy . . .

Claudia Oh! Who lives in Italy?

Tommy Carlotta does.

Claudia Great! I'll write to Karl and Carlotta. I love soccer, and I want to learn German and Italian.

B Read these messages from Tommy's newest e-pals. Write questions and answers. Listen and check. Then practice.

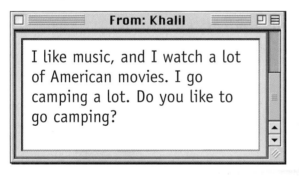

From: Khalil

I like music, and I watch a lot of American movies. I go camping a lot. Do you like to go camping?

From: Christina

I live near beautiful islands. Please visit! You can swim and relax on the beach. I like music. I play the guitar and the piano.

1. Who lives near beautiful islands? *Christina does.*

2. Who watches American movies? _____

3. Who plays the guitar? _____

4. _____ Khalil does.

5. _____ Both Christina and Khalil do.

3. Listening

Tommy talks about his e-pals, Ivan, Emilia, and Christina. Who does these things? Listen and check (✓) the correct name or names.

	Ivan	Emilia	Christina
1. take photographs	☐	☐	☐
2. speak four languages	☐	☐	☐
3. swim every day	☐	☐	☐
4. play the guitar	☐	☐	☐

The Natural World 107

Lesson 39 International Day

1. Numbers 101 +

🔊 **A** Listen and practice.

100 one hundred	154 one hundred and fifty-four
1,000 one thousand	2,000 two thousand
10,000 ten thousand	25,000 twenty-five thousand
100,000 one hundred thousand	960,102 nine hundred sixty thousand, one hundred and two

🔊 **B** Listen and practice.

1,504   6,608   4,412   15,540   60,000   40,420

2. Vocabulary

🔊 **A** Listen and practice.

☐ 154   ☐ 17,000   ☐ 20,000   ☑ 25,000   ☐ 90,000   ☐ 100,000

🔊 **B** This Sunday is International Day at school. Students are giving presentations. Listen and complete their sentences with the correct numbers from the box in part A.

1. Every year, _25,000_ people run from Sydney to Bondi Beach in the Fun Run.

2. There are _____ kinds of birds in my country.

3. There are _____ people in the city of Guaynabo.

4. _____ people can watch a soccer game in Maracanã Stadium.

5. There are _____ national forests in the United States.

6. There are _____ "Mounties" – a special group of police officers – in Canada.

3. Language focus

◁》 **A** Zach's father, Mr. Baker, asks Claudia some questions. Listen and practice.

Mr. Baker	Great presentation, Claudia! Are there really 17,000 species of birds in the Colombian rain forest?
Claudia	At least! Some scientists think there are 20,000. And there are 130,000 species of plants.
Mr. Baker	You know a lot, Claudia! What school subjects do you like?
Claudia	I like math and science.
Mr. Baker	And Zach says you're athletic. What sports do you play?
Claudia	Well, I play soccer, Ping-Pong, basketball, tennis, . . .
Mr. Baker	Wow! And your brother? What sports does he like?
Claudia	He doesn't like sports.
Mr. Baker	What about your parents? What sports do they play?
Claudia	Well, they play tennis and golf. My father plays golf 365 days a year!

> **What + (noun) . . . ?**
> **What subjects** do you like?
> I like math and science.
> **What sports** does he like?
> He doesn't like sports.
> **What sports** do they play?
> They play all sports.

◁》 **B** Now Mr. Baker talks with Rafael. Complete their conversation. Listen and check. Then practice.

Mr. Baker	_What sports_ do you like, Rafael?
Rafael	I like soccer, tennis, and basketball. How about you? _____ , Mr. Baker?
Mr. Baker	Oh, I like all sports, especially baseball.
Rafael	I want to introduce you to my father, but his English isn't very good.
Mr. Baker	_____ speak? Portuguese?
Rafael	Yes. _____ Portuguese and some Spanish.
Mr. Baker	Great! I speak a little Spanish, too. Let's find him!

4. Speaking

Ask your classmates questions. Use the words in the box or your own ideas.

> **colors** music groups **subjects** video games
> foods sports *TV shows*

> What sports do you like?   I like basketball.

The Natural World 109

1. Reading

Do you like storms? Do you think they're beautiful or scary?

What do you do when it's very rainy and windy? Do you go outside? Storm chasers do! Storm chasers are people who follow storms in cars. Most storm chasers want to see tornadoes. A tornado is a strong, fast windstorm. It's tall and spins in a circle.

Storm chasers can be men or women, young or old. Most of them live in the Great Plains in the U.S. – that's where the most storms are. Storm chasers can follow 50 or 60 storms in one year and not see a tornado. But, if they are lucky, storm chasers can see 10 or more tornadoes in one day!

Storm chasers listen to radio and television weather reports, and they read weather maps. They are good at science, and they know a lot about weather. And they are patient.

Why do they chase storms? For scientific information – and because they think storms are exciting and beautiful. Storm chasers like weather, and they like danger, too.

A Read the article about storm chasers.

B Circle the correct word or phrase to complete each sentence.

1. Storm chasers follow storms in (boats / cars).

2. Storm chasers want to (see / stop) tornadoes.

3. Most storms (are / are not) in the Great Plains.

4. Storm chasers (listen to / read) weather reports.

5. Lucky storm chasers can see (10 / 50) tornadoes in one day.

6. Storm chasers are good at (sports / science).

7. They think tornadoes are (awesome / weird).

2. Listening

🔊 **What is the weather like in these cities? Listen and check (✓) the correct information.**

	sunny	warm	cool	cloudy	rainy	windy
1. Valley View	☐	☐	☐	☐	☐	☐
2. Port Harbor	☐	☐	☐	☐	☐	☐
3. Forest Hills	☐	☐	☐	☐	☐	☐
4. Springfield	☐	☐	☐	☐	☐	☐

3. Writing

A **What's the weather usually like this time of year where you live? Check (✓) the words.**

☐ sunny   ☐ cloudy   ☐ rainy
☐ snowy   ☐ windy   ☐ hot
☐ warm   ☐ cool   ☐ cold

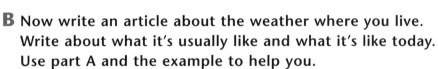

B **Now write an article about the weather where you live. Write about what it's usually like and what it's like today. Use part A and the example to help you.**

I live in Hawaii. In the summer, it's usually hot and sunny. It usually doesn't rain. I like the weather in the summer, but today the weather is weird. It's warm and rainy.

Review

Language chart review

Who + (verb) . . . ?	*What* + (noun) . . . ?
Who goes camping a lot?	**What colors** do you like?
I **do**.	I like blue and yellow.
Pablo **does**.	**What languages** does he speak?
Sarah and Tim **do**.	He speaks French and Italian.

A Look at the pictures. Write questions and answers about the comic book characters.

Magnum

Mira

Katrina and Michael

Danu

Kegar and Magnum

Mira

1. speak English
   Q: *Who speaks English?*　　　A: *Magnum does.*
2. have a pet monkey
   Q: _____　　　A: _____
3. eat a lot of bananas
   Q: _____　　　A: _____
4. live on Earth
   Q: _____　　　A: _____
5. like to play spaceball
   Q: _____　　　A: _____
6. collect comic books
   Q: _____　　　A: _____

B Look again at part A. Write *What* questions with the words.
Then answer the questions.

1. fruit / Mira / like
   Q: *What fruit does Mira like?*   A: *She likes bananas.*
2. instrument / Danu / play
   Q: _____   A: _____
3. café / Katrina and Michael / like
   Q: _____   A: _____
4. languages / Magnum / speak
   Q: _____   A: _____
5. sport / Mira / play
   Q: _____   A: _____
6. color / Kegar and Magnum / like
   Q: _____   A: _____

Language chart review

What's the weather like?	*can* (for possibility)
What's the weather like? It's usually **sunny**.	What **can you** do here? **You can** go hiking.
What's the weather like? It's **cool** and **rainy**.	**Can you** see any animals? Yes, **you can**. / No, **you can't**.

C Katrina asks Kegar about Andor. Look again at the language
chart. Then complete the conversation.

Katrina Hi, Kegar. Do you like Earth?

Kegar Yes, I do. But I miss Andor.

Katrina What's it like there? What *can you* do on Andor?

Kegar A lot of things! It's a great planet for people
who like the outdoors.

Katrina _____ the weather _____ on Andor?

Kegar Well, it's usually cold. Actually, it's really,
really cold!

Katrina Wow! _____ see there?

Kegar _____ see the ice caves. They're
really beautiful.

Katrina What _____ do there?

Kegar _____ visit the Andor School of
Space Travel. That's my school.

Katrina What _____ see at the school?

Kegar _____ see our student spaceships and our
spaceball courts.

Katrina I really want to visit Andor, Kegar.

Kegar Good! Don't forget to bring your coat and hat!

Theme Project: Make a poster about your likes and dislikes.
Themes: Ethics; citizenship
Goal: To create stronger relationships within your classroom community

Prepare

Complete the chart. Then draw or find pictures of the things in the chart. Bring them to class.

Things I like	Things I don't like

Create

Paste the pictures on a piece of paper to make a poster of your likes and dislikes. Use the sample poster as a model.

Write about your likes and dislikes. Do not write your name on the poster.

Present

Read all the posters for your group. Try to guess who made each one. Finally, write the correct names on the posters.

Read the information to another group. Have the group guess who made each poster.

> I like tennis and math. I don't like . . .

> Is it Julia?

Display the posters on the board. Walk around and look at the things your classmates like and dislike.

Things I like   Things I don't like

I like tennis and math. I don't like football at all. I don't like hamburgers. I like dogs a lot!

_____
(name)

Sample poster

Theme Project: Make a routine chart for a person in another class.
Theme: Citizenship
Goal: To become better acquainted with your school community

Prepare

Look at the chart. Each group member chooses a student in another class to interview. Complete the chart with questions about routines.

Student:	
Morning	*Do you eat breakfast at home?*
Afternoon	
Evening	
Free time	*Do you listen to music?*

Create

Interview the student. Write about the student's routine. Use the sample routine chart as a model.

Student:	*Diane Crane*
Morning	*She gets up at 7:00. She doesn't eat breakfast at home.*
Afternoon	*She doesn't go home at 3:00. She does her homework at 4:00.*
Evening	*She doesn't eat dinner with her friends. She goes to bed at 10:00.*
Free time	*She doesn't listen to music. She hangs out at the mall.*

Sample chart

Present

Tell your group about your student.

> Diane gets up at 7:00. She doesn't . . .

Display the routine charts in the classroom. Walk around and look at them.

Theme Project: Make a sports card.
Themes: Cultural diversity; health
Goal: To learn about sports in different countries.

Prepare

Your teacher will assign a country for you to research. Complete the chart.
Then find information about two or three popular sports in that country.

Country	Popular sports	Information
	1. _____	_____
_____	2. _____	_____
	3. _____	_____

Create

Choose the most interesting sport. Make a card for that sport. Use the
sample card as a model. Bring the card to class.

Present

Trade cards with group members.
Don't show your card to your group
members. Ask and answer questions.
Try to guess the countries and sports
on the cards.

Do they wear uniforms?

Yes, they do.

Display the cards on the board.
Walk around and look at them.

People in Canada play ice hockey.
Ice hockey players wear uniforms.
They wear helmets.
They play on a skating rink.

Sample card

Theme Project: Make a song poster.
Theme: Cultural diversity
Goals: To stimulate creativity; to become acquainted with music from other countries

Prepare

Read the song lyrics assigned to your group by the teacher. Look up new words in the dictionary. Cut pictures from magazines or draw pictures to illustrate the song. Bring them to class.

Create

Paste the pictures for your song on a big piece of paper to make a poster. Write the name of the song at the top of the poster. Write some of the lyrics of the song on the poster. Use the sample poster as a model.

Present

Tell another group about your song.

> This is a famous song. I like it a lot.

Sing the song for the other group.

Display the posters around the classroom. Choose your favorite poster.

The Water Is Wide

There is a ship,
and she sails the sea.
She is as deep,
as deep as can be.

Sample poster

UNIT 5

Theme Project: Make a city guide for tourists.
Theme: Citizenship
Goals: To increase your knowledge of your city or town; to provide useful information for visitors

Prepare

What are some interesting places to visit in your town or city? Choose two places in each category. Complete the chart. Find pictures of activities people do in those places. Bring them to class.

Town / City: _____

Parks	Museums	Other favorite places
Central Park		

Create

Choose the three best places. Make a page for each place on a piece of paper. Write two or three activities visitors can do in each place. Use the sample page as a model.

Make a guide. Staple all the pages together. Make a cover.

Present

Tell another group about the things that people are doing in the pictures in your guide.

> Some people are having a picnic. They are . . .

Display the guides in the classroom. Vote on the class's favorite places to visit.

Sample page

UNIT 6

Theme Project: Make a group guide of favorite weekend activities.
Themes: Relationships; citizenship
Goal: To create stronger relationships within your classroom community

Prepare

Look at the chart. Each group member chooses a different weekend activity. Choose an activity from the box or use your own ideas.

Weekend activities			
eat at a restaurant	go to the movies	play a sport	other _____
go to a concert	play cards	relax at home	

Create

Draw or find pictures or advertisements to illustrate your activity. Make a page for your activity. Use the sample page as a model. Write your name on your page. Bring the page to class.

Show your page to your group. Staple all the pages together to make a guide. Make a cover.

Present

Show your guide to another group. Talk about your group's favorite activities.

> We like to go to concerts. This weekend we want to see the Red Hot Chili Peppers. They're great!

Display the guides in the classroom. Walk around and look at the guides. Find another classmate who likes the same activity. Talk about that activity.

> I like to listen to music. I have a lot of CDs at home.

> I like to listen to music, too. Laura Pausini is my favorite singer.

Go to a concert

Marcos Oliveira

Sample page

Theme Project: Make a group menu.
Theme: Health and healthy foods
Goal: To share information about healthy foods and snacks

Prepare

Your teacher will assign each member of your group breakfast, lunch, after-school snack, or dinner. Choose a healthy food to eat for your meal. Draw or find pictures of that food. Bring the pictures to class.

Create

Show your pictures to your group. Make a group menu with the pictures. Write the names of the meals and the healthy food items. Use the sample menu as a model.

Present

Display the menus on the board.
Walk around and look at them.
Talk to classmates about the menus.
Talk about the things on your menu.

> My meal is lunch. I eat a sandwich. On the sandwich, there's some ham, a little mustard, and a lot of lettuce. I drink . . .

Sample menu

Theme Project: Make an informational guide about a different continent.
Theme: Cultural diversity
Goal: To learn about different countries around the world

Prepare

Your teacher will assign a continent for your group to research. Each group member chooses a different country on that continent.

Complete the chart. Draw or find pictures that show people, cities, famous places, sports, and weather from the country you chose. Bring the chart and pictures to class.

Country: _____

Continent: _____

Important city: _____

Weather in that city: _____

Famous place: _____

Popular sports: _____

Create

Make a page about your country on a piece of paper. Use the sample page as a model.

Show your page to your group. Ask and answer questions about your group's countries.

> What sports do Peruvians play?

> They play soccer, volleyball, and basketball.

Make a group continent guide. Staple all the pages together. Make a cover.

Present

Show your guide to another group.

Display the guides in the classroom. Vote on the most interesting guide.

Peru

Peru is in South America.

Lima is an important city in Peru. It's usually hot and sunny in Lima.

Machu Picchu is a famous place in Peru.

Peruvians play soccer, volleyball, and basketball.

Sample page

My Learning Log: Unit 1

A Complete questions 1 and 2. Answer them with your own information. Write three more questions with the verb *be*. Then answer the questions.

1. **Q:** _____ your name?   **A:** _____

2. **Q:** _____ are you from?   **A:** _____

3. **Q:** _____   **A:** _____

4. **Q:** _____   **A:** _____

5. **Q:** _____   **A:** _____

B Complete number 1. Then write three questions and complete the answers for numbers 2–4. Use *is*, *are*, *isn't*, or *aren't*.

1. **Q:** _____ there a library in your neighborhood?   **A:** Yes, _____ .

2. **Q:** _____   **A:** No, _____ .

3. **Q:** _____   **A:** Yes, _____ .

4. **Q:** _____   **A:** No, _____ .

C Complete number 1. Then write sentences for numbers 2–4. Use *like* or *don't like* with *a lot*, *a little*, *very much*, or *at all*.

1. I like _____ a lot.

2. _____

3. _____

4. _____

D Write sentences about people you know. What are they good at? What are their talents? Complete numbers 1 and 2. Then write sentences for numbers 3 and 4.

1. _____ is good at _____ . She's really _____ .

2. _____ not good at _____ . He's not _____ .

3. _____

4. _____

E Complete the sentences about yourself.

1. Two exciting places in my town / city are _____ .

2. I like _____ . They're cute animals.

F Review your work in Unit 1. Complete the sentences.

1. One interesting new thing I learned in this unit is _____ .

2. One important thing I reviewed in this unit is _____ .

My Learning Log: Unit 2

A Complete number 1. Then write sentences for numbers 2–4.
Use a different verb for each item.

1. I ___*live*___ in a house. I _____ in an apartment.

2. He _____ . _____ .

3. She _____ . _____ .

4. He _____ . _____ .

B Complete numbers 1 and 2. Then complete the questions and
write the answers for numbers 3 and 4.

1. **Q:** _____ you _____ your homework every day?   **A:** Yes, _____ .

2. **Q:** _____ you _____ lunch in the cafeteria?   **A:** No, _____ .

3. **Q:** _____ you _____ ?   **A:** _____

4. **Q:** _____ you _____ ?   **A:** _____

C Write the words in the box next to the correct verbs or verb
phrases. Then add one more word to each list.

☐ breakfast   ☐ e-mail messages   ☐ letters   ☐ the piano
☐ dinner   ☐ home   ☐ soccer   ☐ to bed

eat   _____   _____   _____

go   _____   _____   _____

play _____   _____   _____

write _____   _____   _____

D Complete the sentences about yourself.

1. Two things I do in the morning are _____

_____ .

2. Two things I don't do in the morning are _____

_____ .

3. Two things I do on the weekend are _____

_____ .

E Review your work in Unit 2. Complete the sentences.

1. An easy exercise for me is Exercise _____ on page _____ .

2. A difficult exercise for me is Exercise _____ on page _____ .

3. Three important new words from this unit are _____

My Learning Log: Unit 3

A Complete numbers 1 and 2. Then write your own questions and answers for numbers 3 and 4. For number 3, write about your best friend. For number 4, write about a person you admire. Use *he* or *she.*

1. **Q:** _____ Chris like sports?   **A:** No, he _____ .

2. **Q:** _____ Claudia _____ basketball?   **A:** Yes, _____ .

3. **Q:** _____   **A:** _____

4. **Q:** _____   **A:** _____

B Complete number 1. Then write questions and answers for numbers 2 and 3. For number 2, write about athletes. For number 3, write about friends or family. Use *they.*

1. **Q:** _____ soccer players wear helmets?   **A:** No, _____ .

2. **Q:** _____   **A:** Yes, _____ .

3. **Q:** _____   **A:** _____

C Complete numbers 1 and 2. Then write sentences for numbers 3–6. Write about four rules at your school.

1. _____ in English class.   4. _____

2. Don't _____ in English class.   5. _____

3. _____   6. _____

D Write sentences with the times you do the things in numbers 2 and 3. Use *in the morning, in the afternoon, in the evening,* or *at night.*

1. *I get up at 7:00.* _____ (get up)

2. _____ (go to school)

3. _____ (do homework)

E Write sentences about yourself.

1. A rule I like: _____

2. A rule I don't like: _____

F Review your work in Unit 3. Complete the sentences.

1. My favorite part of this unit is Exercise _____ on page _____ .

2. Three difficult words for me are _____ .

3. What do you think? Circle the words. This unit is (boring / difficult / easy / exciting / fun / funny / important / interesting).

My Learning Log: Unit 4

A Circle your opinions and complete the sentences in numbers 1 and 2. Then write sentences for numbers 3 and 4. Write about a singer, a musical group, a sports team, or other people you know.

1. Jazz is (great / boring). I (like / don't like) _____ .

2. Madonna is (weird / cool). I (like / don't like) _____ .

3. _____

4. _____

B Complete numbers 1 and 2. Then write a question and an answer for number 3.

1. **Q:** How much _____ this video game?   **A:** _____ $29.99.

2. **Q:** _____ those sneakers?   **A:** _____ $65.00.

3. **Q:** _____   **A:** _____

C Write the words in the box in the correct list. Then add two more words to each column.

☐ rock   ☐ video set   ☐ space map
☐ camping   ☐ hip-hop   ☐ dancing

Free-time activities	Music	Catalog items
_____ _____	_____ _____	_____ _____
_____ _____	_____ _____	_____ _____

D Complete numbers 1 and 2. Then write sentences for numbers 3 and 4. Use *like to* or *don't like to*.

1. I like to _____ .   3. _____

2. I don't like to _____ .   4. _____

E Write sentences about yourself.

1. A friend I always hang out with: _____

2. The place I usually go to after school: _____

3. An expensive thing I never buy: _____

F Review your work in Unit 4. Complete the sentences.

1. An important new question from this unit is _____ .

2. My favorite conversation in this unit is on page _____ .

3. What do you think? Circle the words. This unit is (boring / cool / difficult / easy / exciting / fun / funny / great / important / interesting / weird).

My Learning Log: Unit 5

A Complete number 1. Then write present continuous sentences for numbers 2–5.

1. I'm _____ my homework right now. I'm not _____ .

2. _____ (you) _____

3. _____ (he) _____

4. _____ (she) _____

5. _____ (they) _____

B Complete number 1. Then write three questions and answers for numbers 2–4.

1. **Q:** _____ you standing in line right now? **A:** No, _____ . I'm _____ .

2. **Q:** _____ (he) **A:** _____

3. **Q:** _____ (she) **A:** _____

4. **Q:** _____ (they) **A:** _____

C Complete numbers 1 and 2. Then write three questions and answers for numbers 3–5.

1. **Q:** What _____ you doing? **A:** I'm _____ .

2. **Q:** _____ reading? **A:** She's _____ .

3. **Q:** _____ (he) **A:** _____

4. **Q:** _____ (we) **A:** _____

5. **Q:** _____ (they) **A:** _____

D Write these words in the correct web. Then add one more word or phrase to each web.

☐ a baseball   ☐ a boat ride   ☐ a bracelet   ☐ clothes   ☐ a Frisbee® disc   ☐ pictures

THROWING

TAKING

TRYING ON

E Review your work in Unit 5. Complete the sentences.

1. There's some important information in Exercise _____ on page _____ .

2. There's a funny conversation in Exercise _____ on page _____ .

3. What do you think? Circle the words. This unit is (boring / difficult / easy / exciting / fun / funny / important / interesting).

My Learning Log: Unit 6

A Complete number 1. Then write four questions and answers for numbers 2–5.

1. **Q:** Where ___are___ you ___going___ now?   **A:** I'm _____ .

2. **Q:** _____ (he)   **A:** _____

3. **Q:** _____ (she)   **A:** _____

4. **Q:** _____ (we)   **A:** _____

5. **Q:** _____ (they)   **A:** _____

B Complete numbers 1 and 2. Then write sentences for numbers 3–5.

1. Right now I _____ . _____ usually _____ .

2. Usually my friends _____ . Today, _____ .

3. _____

4. _____

5. _____

C Complete numbers 1–4. Then write questions and answers for numbers 5 and 6.

1. I want to _____ this weekend.

2. I don't want _____ .

3. **Q:** Do _____ want to _____ ?   **A:** _____

4. **Q:** What _____ want _____ ?   **A:** _____

5. **Q:** _____   **A:** _____

6. **Q:** _____   **A:** _____

D Answer the questions about yourself.

1. What do you look like?

_____

2. What does your best friend look like?

_____

E Review your work in Unit 6. Complete the sentences.

1. Three easy phrases for me are _____ .

2. Three difficult phrases for me are _____ .

3. What do you think? Circle the words. This unit is (amazing / awesome / boring / cool / difficult / easy / exciting / fun / funny / great / important / interesting / weird).

My Learning Log: Unit 7

A Complete numbers 1 and 2. Then write a question and an answer for number 3.

1. **Q:** How many _____ do you eat every day?

   A: I eat _____ . I like _____ a lot.

2. **Q:** How much _____ does your family eat every week?

   A: We eat _____ . We don't like _____ very much.

3. **Q:** _____

   A: _____

B Complete numbers 1 and 2. Then write a sentence for number 3.

1. There are some _____ in my classroom, but there aren't

   any _____ .

2. I have some _____ , but I don't have any _____ .

3. _____

C Write about the food you would like for dinner tonight. Use *I'd like*.

_____

D You want to make a meal for your friends. What do you need? Complete the sentences with *some, a few, a little,* or *a lot of*. Use the words in the box or your own ideas.

bread	butter	ham	mayonnaise	pepper	rice	vegetables
broccoli	cheese	lettuce	mustard		potatoes	salt	water

For the soup, I need

_____

For the sandwiches, I need

_____

E Write about yourself. Use *have* and *a lot of, a little, a few, some, any,* or a number.

1. Friends: _____

2. Cousins: _____

3. Books: _____

F Review your work in Unit 7. Complete the sentences.

1. My favorite part of the unit is Exercise _____ on page _____ .

2. Three easy words for me are _____ .

My Learning Log: Unit 8

A Complete numbers 1 and 2. Then write a question and an answer for number 3.

1. **Q:** _____ the weather _____ in _____ in _____ ?

(place)   (month)

   A: _____

2. **Q:** _____ weather _____ today?

   A: _____

3. **Q:** _____

   A: _____

B Complete the first questions in numbers 1 and 2 with places you know. Then write questions and answers.

1. **Q:** _____ can you _____ in _____ ? **A:** You can _____ .

   Q: Can you _____ ? **A:** Yes, _____ .

   Q: _____ ? **A:** No, _____ .

2. **Q:** _____ can you _____ in _____ ? **A:** _____

   Q: _____ **A:** _____

   Q: _____ **A:** _____

C Think about your friends, your family, and yourself. Complete numbers 1 and 2. Then write a question and an answer for number 3.

1. **Q:** Who lives _____ ? **A:** _____ does.

2. **Q:** Who _____ ? **A:** _____ do.

3. **Q:** _____ **A:** _____

D Complete the questions in numbers 1 and 2, and answer them. Then write a question and an answer for number 3.

1. **Q:** What _____ do you like? **A:** _____

2. **Q:** _____ does _____ ? **A:** _____

3. **Q:** _____ **A:** _____

E Review your work in Units 1–8. Write sentences about yourself.

1. My talents: _____

2. Things I do in my free time: _____

3. Activities I never do: _____

4. Things I'm doing now: _____

5. A movie I want to see: _____

Word List

This word list includes the new words and phrases in Connect Student's Book 2.
Vocabulary items are listed with the number of the lesson in which a word first appears.

Key Vocabulary

A a

action movie (28) _____
active (4) _____
activities (13) _____
admire (8) _____
adult (26) _____
adventure DVDs (17) _____
after (6) _____
afternoon [in the . . .] (14) _____
again (13) _____
age (18) _____
all [at all] (4) _____
almost (17) _____
amazing (26) _____
animated movie (28) _____
answer (19) _____
appetizer (34) _____
apple (31) _____
Arabic (38) _____
artistic (3) _____
arts and crafts (14) _____
at home (9) _____
At least! (39) _____
at night (13) _____
athlete (26) _____
athletic (3) _____
attention (22) _____
average (29) _____
awesome (26) _____

B b

baby (23) _____
baked potato (34) _____
ball (23) _____
banana (31) _____
barbecue (27) _____
baseball bat (24) _____
baseball player (12) _____
basketball court (2) _____
bass (8) _____
bat [animal] (26) _____
bathing suit (23) _____
beans (34) _____
bear (37) _____
belt (24) _____
bike path (22) _____

biking (11) _____
bird (37) _____
black bean soup (34) _____
blanket (13) _____
blond (29) _____
boat (22) _____
boat ride (21) _____
body (type) (29) _____
both (39) _____
bowling (19) _____
bracelet (24) _____
bread (32) _____
breakfast (6) _____
bring (13) _____
broccoli (31) _____
bug repellent (13) _____
busy (14) _____
butter (31) _____
buy (21) _____

C c

cake (27) _____
camp (13) _____
campers (14) _____
campfire (14) _____
camping (18) _____
canoeing (14) _____
cards (27) _____
carrot cake (34) _____
cat (4) _____
catalog (17) _____
cave (37) _____
celebrate (27) _____
cents (17) _____
checklist (13) _____
cheese (31) _____
cheeseburger (34) _____
chicken sandwich (34) _____
chocolate cake (34) _____
circus (26) _____
climb (37) _____
clothes (8) _____
clothing (8) _____
cloudy (36) _____
coat (24) _____
cold (36) _____

collect (7) _____
come (19) _____
comedy (28) _____
comfortable (13) _____
cook (14) _____
cookie (31) _____
cool (36) _____
country (music) (16) _____
court [sports] (12) _____
crossword puzzles (18) _____
cup (32) _____
curly (29) _____
cyclist (12) _____

D d

dance lessons (7) _____
dancing (18) _____
dangerous (4) _____
dessert (34) _____
different (9) _____
diner (34) _____
dinner (6) _____
documentary (28) _____
dog (4) _____
dollars (17) _____
drama (28) _____
dress (13) _____
drinks [noun] (32) _____
DVD (7) _____

E e

each (17) _____
early (13) _____
eat (6) _____
eat out (9) _____
egg (31) _____
egg sandwich (31) _____
electric keyboard (8) _____
else (32) _____
e-mail messages (6) _____
end (29) _____
especially (39) _____
evening [in the . . .] (14) _____
everyone (36) _____
everything (24) _____
exhibit (26) _____

expensive (17) _____

experiment kit (17) _____

eye (12) _____

F f

fascinating (26) _____

fashion designer (8) _____

feet (12) _____

few [a few] (32) _____

find (38) _____

fish (34) _____

flashlight (13) _____

float (23) _____

fly (23) _____

follow (22) _____

foot (12) _____

for a change (31) _____

forget (37) _____

fork (32) _____

free time (7) _____

french fries (34) _____

Frisbee® disc (23) _____

fruit (32) _____

G g

German (38) _____

Germany (38) _____

get up (6) _____

glove(s) (12) _____

goggles (12) _____

golf (39) _____

Good! (33) _____

good (at something) (3) _____

grades (19) _____

Greece (38) _____

Greek (38) _____

group (16) _____

guess (8) _____

guy (11) _____

H h

hair (29) _____

hairstyle (29) _____

ham (33) _____

ham sandwich (33) _____

hand (12) _____

hang out (7) _____

hard [work hard] (8) _____

hardly ever (19) _____

hate (26) _____

head (12) _____

headphones (19) _____

healthy (31) _____

heavy (29) _____

height (29) _____

helmet (12) _____

help (11) _____

help [noun] (36) _____

high school [adjective] (8) _____

hike (14) _____

hiking boots (13) _____

him (16) _____

hip-hop (music) (16) _____

horror movie (28) _____

horseback riding (14) _____

hot spring (37) _____

hotel (37) _____

houseboat (37) _____

how [How old is he?] (1) _____

I i

ice cream (31) _____

iced tea (34) _____

idea (33) _____

incredible (26) _____

information (36) _____

in line (22) _____

in-line (skate) (7) _____

instrument (3) _____

interests (18) _____

Internet (7) _____

introduce (39) _____

island (37) _____

Italy (38) _____

J j

jazz (16) _____

jazz band (8) _____

jazz club (8) _____

jelly (33) _____

jewelry (24) _____

jokes (3) _____

juice (32) _____

just a minute (13) _____

K k

karate (11) _____

ketchup (33) _____

kind [what kind of] (16) _____

kite (23) _____

knee (12) _____

knee pad(s) (12) _____

knives [*sing.* knife] (32) _____

L l

language (3) _____

learn (26) _____

leave (13) _____

lesson (6) _____

lettuce (33) _____

lifeguard chair (23) _____

light (22) _____

line [in line] (22) _____

listen (7) _____

long (29) _____

look (like) (29) _____

M m

main dish (34) _____

make (3) _____

man (23) _____

many [how many] (32) _____

maybe (17) _____

mayonnaise (33) _____

meat (31) _____

medium-length (29) _____

menu (34) _____

messy (4) _____

midnight (13) _____

milk (32) _____

milk shake (34) _____

morning [in the . . .] (14) _____

Morocco (38) _____

mountain (37) _____

movie (1) _____

much [adjective] (16) _____

much [how much] (17) _____

much [very much] (4) _____

musical (3) _____

musician (16) _____

mustard (33) _____

N n

national forest (39) _____

Nature Center (26) _____

nature puzzles (17) _____

near (23) _____

necklace (24) _____

need (12) _____

never (19) _____

No kidding! (12) _____

nothing (31) _____

numbers [101+] (39) _____

O o

ocean (23) _____

off (to) (13) _____

one hundred and two (39) _____

one hundred thousand (39) _____

one thousand (39) _____

on time (19) _____

open (27) _____

or (6) _____

order (34) _____

outdoors (18) _____

over (8) _____

own [his own] (8) _____

P p

paper airplanes (19) _____
parrot (4) _____
party game (27) _____
pasta (32) _____
pay (attention) (22) _____
pay for (24) _____
people (8) _____
pepper (33) _____
person (18) _____
photograph (38) _____
piano lesson (7) _____
picnic area (22) _____
picture (3) _____
pie (34) _____
pillow (13) _____
plan [noun] (32) _____
plant [noun] (39) _____
plate (32) _____
play (3) _____
poetry (18) _____
police officer (39) _____
pop (music) (16) _____
popcorn (9) _____
popular (26) _____
Portuguese (38) _____
potato (31) _____
practice (8) _____
present [noun] (27) _____
presentation (39) _____
pretty (good at) (3) _____

Q q

question (19) _____

R r

rabbit (4) _____
radio-controlled airplane (17) _____
raft (23) _____
raincoat (13) _____
rain forest (37) _____
rainy (36) _____
read (13) _____
Really? (16) _____
refrigerator (31) _____
reggae (music) (16) _____
relax (27) _____
rice (31) _____
ride (21) _____
ring (24) _____
river (37) _____
robot (26) _____
rules (22) _____
run (39) _____

Russia (38) _____
Russian (38) _____

S s

sail (23) _____
salad (34) _____
salt (33) _____
sand (23) _____
say (13) _____
scarf (24) _____
science homework (36) _____
scientist (39) _____
sea (37) _____
seashells (23) _____
shop (24) _____
shopping (18) _____
side order (34) _____
sightseeing (21) _____
skate (7) _____
skateboarder (12) _____
ski (11) _____
ski boot(s) (12) _____
skier (12) _____
sleep (9) _____
sleeping bag (13) _____
slim (29) _____
slow (27) _____
snack (33) _____
snowy (36) _____
soap (13) _____
soccer (1) _____
soccer practice (19) _____
something (13) _____
song (26) _____
sound (36) _____
sound (like) (14) _____
souvenir (21) _____
souvenir shop (37) _____
space map (17) _____
special (39) _____
species (39) _____
spend (18) _____
spider (4) _____
spoon (32) _____
sports (1) _____
sports equipment (12) _____
sports star (11) _____
stadium (39) _____
stamps (7) _____
stand (22) _____
start (29) _____
stay (home) (9) _____
stay on (22) _____
stay up (9) _____

steak sandwich (34) _____
stop (13) _____
stories (14) _____
straight (29) _____
student (8) _____
study (24) _____
subject (39) _____
sunny (36) _____
sunscreen (13) _____
supplies (32) _____
supposed (to be) (13) _____
sure (28) _____
Sure! (12) _____
surf (11) _____
surfboard (24) _____
surprise (26) _____
survey (7) _____
swim (11) _____
swimming (18) _____
swimming lessons (14) _____
swim team (12) _____

T t

take (7) _____
talented (8) _____
talk (7) _____
teach (8) _____
temperature (36) _____
tennis (1) _____
tennis racket (24) _____
ten thousand (39) _____
them (16) _____
then (6) _____
there [Hello there!] (1) _____
thrilling (26) _____
throw (19) _____
today's [adjective] (34) _____
tonight (27) _____
too bad (17) _____
towel (13) _____
trail (37) _____
trash (22) _____
trash can (22) _____
travel vest (17) _____
trip (21) _____
trolley (21) _____
try on (24) _____
twenty-five thousand (39) _____
two thousand (39) _____

U u

underground (37) _____
until (13) _____
us (29) _____

use (7) _____

usually (19) _____

V v

vegetable soup (34) _____

video (7) _____

video sets (17) _____

videotape [verb] (21) _____

violin lesson (6) _____

visit (21) _____

W w

wait (for) (22) _____

walk (21) _____

wall calendar (17) _____

want (28) _____

warm (36) _____

watch (6) _____

water (31) _____

water-ski (11) _____

wavy (29) _____

wear (12) _____

weather (36) _____

Web site (17) _____

week (8) _____

weekend (7) _____

windy (36) _____

wolves [*sing.* wolf] (37) _____

woman (29) _____

work (8) _____

world (8) _____

would (34) _____

Acknowledgments

The authors and publisher would like to thank the following teachers and pilot schools for their feedback and suggestions during the development of *Connect*:

Regina Coeli Baldin Saponara, **Colégio Nossa Senhora de Sion,** Brazil; Angela Maria Grattoni Moreira, **Colégio Penha de França,** Brazil; Ana Lúcia Cabral Amancio, **Colégio Santa Teresinha,** Brazil; Maria Heloisa Alves Audino, **Escola São Teodoro de N. S. de Sion,** Brazil; Andrew Augustine, Simon Butler, and Catherine Milne, **Fujimi Junior and Senior High School,** Catherine Woods, **Fujimura Junior and Senior High School,** Japan; Japan; David Eadon and Tony Fox, **Shumei Junior High School,** Japan

The authors and publisher are extremely grateful to the following teachers who participated in focus groups:

Gordon Sites, **Aikoku Gakuen,** Japan; Natsumi Suzuki, **ALC Education,** Japan; Elisabeth Keene and Margaret Workman, **Bunkyo Junior and Senior High School,** Japan; Katy Cox and Solange Pedroza, **Casa Thomas Jefferson,** Brazil; Silvana Carlini, **Colégio Agostiniano Mendel,** Brazil; Solange Fátima Rey Cabral, **Colégio Alvorecer,** Brazil; Maria Regina Silva Gomes, **Colégio Anglo Americano,** Brazil; Ana Clotilde Thomé, **Colégio Batista Brasileiro,** Brazil; Maria Cláudia C. F. Souza, **Colégio da Cidade,** Brazil; Cláudia Thereza Mendes, **Colégio Franco Brasileiro,** Brazil; Glória Elena Pereira Nunes, **Colégio Franco Brasileiro / Colégio Isa Prates,** Brazil; Noraide Maria S. M. S. Trindade, **Colégio Max Nordau,** Brazil; Angela Cristina Rodrigues de Castro and Simone Correia Silva, **Colégio Militar,** Brazil; Silvia Gagliardi, **Colégio Moema,** Brazil; Cláudia Ramis de Almeida, **Colégio Rainha da Paz,** Brazil; Marcos Conte, **Colégio Renovação,** Brazil; Robson Silva de Lucena and Adele Vietri, **Colégio Saint Exupery,** Brazil; Nádia Godinho and Sandra Macri Landi Oliveira, **Colégio Salesiano Santa Teresinha,** Brazil; Borrvs W. G. Ferrick, **Dokkyo Junior High School,** Japan; Ann Conlon, **ECC Abenobashi,** Japan; Lilian Vaisman, **Escola Israelita A. Liessin,** Brazil; Tony Collins and Robert Diem, **Fujimura Junior and Senior High School,** Japan; David Smith and Jad Michaelson, **Ganghwa Middle School,** South Korea; Masakazu Kimura, **Gyoshu Junior and Senior High School,** Japan; Júlia França de Lima, **Instituto Educacional Stella Maris,** Brazil; Claudio Lopez, **Joyful English School,** Japan; Paul Gilson, **Keio Fujisawa,** Japan; Phillippe Loussarevian, **Keio SFC Junior High and High School,** Japan; Lee Ji Won and Jeong Kyung Sook (Pix), **Kukdong school branch,** South Korea; Koh Yu-Mee and Sun Hee Yong, **Kun Kuk BCM PLS,** South Korea; Ryan Allen Gjovig, **Sanggye Language School,** South Korea; Harry Ahn and Mike Langley, **Seoul Teacher Training Center,** South Korea; Anita Bonner, **Shane Corporation,** Japan; Adrian Thomas, **Shoei Joshi Gakuin,** Japan; Paula Covacs, **Shumei Eiko Koko,** Japan; Leandro Racco and Daniel Choi, **Snappy Private Language School,** South Korea; Chunggyu Kim, **Sunflower English Academy,** South Korea; Ann Hubert, **Tachibana Junior and Senior High School,** Japan; Ying-Hsiu Ku, **Taipei First Girls Senior High School,** Taiwan; Li-Hsin Jan, **Taipei Municipal Long-Shan Junior High School,** Taiwan;Yin-Mei Huang, **Taipei Municipal Shih Lin Junior High School,** Taiwan; Yi-Zhu Liu and Siao-Ping Chang, **Taipei Municipal Wan Fan High School,** Taiwan; Maria Amélia Marcos, **União Cultural Brasil Estados Unidos,** Brazil Napoleon Fonseca and Norio Kawakubo, **Yokohama YMCA ACT,** Japan; Minton Yang, **Yen-Ping Senior High School,** Taiwan

The authors and publisher are also indebted to Inara Couto, **Cel-Lep,** Brazil; Camilla Dixo Lieff, **PUC,** Brazil; Liani Moraes, **Colégio São Luís,** Brazil; Helena Nagano; and the many teachers who allowed us to observe their classes and who shared so much of their teaching experience with us. Special thanks also go to over 150 teachers in Latin America and Asia who answered questionnaires and reviewed material.

Text Credits

26 "Homeschool." Adapted by permission from Anna Kulczyk.

54 "American Teens and Free Time." Data from *Kidbits*; Blackbirch Press, Inc., 2001

64 *Frisbee* is a registered trademark of Wham-O, Inc.

Illustration Credits

Michael Brennan 42, 43, 76

Andrea Champlin 72, 77, 95

Laurie Conley 50, 51, 52, 63, 64, 65, 98, 99

Bruce Day 16, 24, 56, 70, 80, 81

Adam Hurwitz 52, 78, 83, 100, 101

Jocha 15, 73

Larry Jones 7, 36, 37, 39, 74, 75, 92, 93,

Andrew Shiff 4, 10, 11, 56, 60, 61, 68, 86, 104

Photographic Credits

2, 3, 8, 9, 12, 18, 24, 25, 31, 32, 33, 45, 47, 62, 66, 67, 73, 75, 79, 87, 89, 95, 101, 103, 107, 108, 109 ©Lawrence Migdale

46, 57, 88, 89 ©George Kerrigan

5 *(clockwise from top left)* ©Susan Van Etten/PhotoEdit; ©Photolibrary; ©Yadid Levy/AGE Fotostock; ©Photodisc/Getty Images; ©Ruddy Gold/AGE Fotostock; ©Photodisc/Getty Images; ©Photodisc/Getty Images; ©Tony Freeman/PhotoEdit

6 *(clockwise from top left)* ©Lawrence Migdale; ©Mark Richards/PhotoEdit; ©Rob Gage/Getty Images

13 ©Thinkstock

14 *(clockwise from top left)* ©Dave Nagel/Getty Images; ©Envision; ©Photolibrary

28 ©Grazia Neri/Camera Press/Retna Ltd.; ©Mark Anderson/Retna Ltd.

29 ©Photolibrary

17 *(left to right)* ©Bananastock/Punchstock; ©Jack Hollingsworth/Corbis

22 *(clockwise from top left)* ©John Valls/AGE Fotostock; ©Corbis; ©Kevin Fleming/Corbis; ©Photodisc/Getty Images; ©Ed Bock/Corbis; ©Simon Watson/Getty Images

23 *(top to bottom)* ©Eric McNatt/Retna Ltd.; ©Neal Preston/Corbis

30 *(clockwise from top left)* ©David Pu'u/Corbis; © Comstock; ©Steve Smith/SuperStock; ©Ko Fujiwara/Photonica; ©Mike Chew/Corbis; ©Photodisc/Getty Images; ©Bilderberg/Photonica; ©David Epperson/Getty Images;

32 *(right, top to bottom)* ©Photolibrary; ©Veer; ©Photodisc/Getty Images; ©Veer; ©Photodisc/Getty Images

33 *(bottom, left to right)* ©Duomo/Corbis; ©Nils Johan Norenlind/AGE Fotostock; ©Duomo/Corbis; ©Photodisc/Getty Images

34 ©See Jane Run/Workbook

38 *(clockwise from top left)* ©Yellow Dog Productions/Getty Images; ©Comstock; ©Wilson Goodrich/Index Stock; ©BananaStock/SuperStock; ©Kelly-Mooney Photography/Corbis; ©Carl D. Walsh/Aurora Photos; ©Yellow Dog Productions/Getty Images; ©Phil Schermeister/Corbis

40 *(left to right)* ©Dario Lopez Mills/AP Photo; ©Mark Thompson/Getty Images

41 ©Reuters NewMedia Inc./Corbis

44 *(clockwise from top left)* ©Stanley L. Rowin/Mira.com; ©Matthew Peyton/Getty Images; ©David Atlas/Retna Ltd.; ©Mark Mainz/Getty Images; ©EPA PHOTO/EFE/Gorka Ayestaran/AP Photo; ©ShowBizIreland/Getty Images; ©Carlos Alvarez/Getty Images

48 ©Digital Vision/Getty Images

53 *(left to right)* ©Patrick Altmann/Getty Images; ©Lenora Gim/Photonica; ©Burke/Triolo/Masterfile

54 *(clockwise from top left)* ©Cat Gwynn/Corbis; ©Thinkstock/Getty Images; ©Pedro Coll/AGE Fotostock; ©Photodisc/Getty Images

58 *(clockwise from top left)* ©John Elk III/Lonely Planet; ©Lee Foster/Lonely Planet; ©Bluestone Productions/Getty Images; ©Photolibrary/Photonica; ©Richard Price/Getty Images; ©Corbis; ©Robert Eric/Corbis; ©Digital Vision/Getty Images

59 *(left to right)* ©Terry Vine/Getty Images; ©Mary Crosby/Getty Images; 2 others ©Lawrence Migdale

68 *(left, top to bottom)* ©Francisco Cruz/SuperStock; ©Richard I'Anson/Lonely Planet; *(middle, top to bottom)* ©Rob Flynn/Lonely Planet; ©Curzon Studio/Envision; *(right)* ©Photodisc/Creatas

69 *(top to bottom)* ©Corbis Sygma; ©Dave Bartruff/Corbis; ©David Ball/Index Stock

78 *(clockwise from top left)* ©Peter Beavis/Getty Images; ©Lisette Le Bon/SuperStock; ©Carl Fischer/Mira.com; ©David Keaton/Corbis; ©Jon Feingersh/Masterfile

93 *(clockwise from top left)* ©George Kerrigan; ©Foodcollection/Stockfood; ©George Kerrigan; ©Photodisc; ©George Kerrigan; ©Artville; ©Photodisc; ©Burke/Triolo Productions/Getty Images

94 *(top, left to right)* ©Thom DeSanto Photography, Inc./Stockfood; ©Rita Maas/Getty Images; ©Artville; ©Susie M.

Notes

Notes

Notes

Notes